CHINA SIMPLIFIED

History Flashback

An entertaining journey through the past
to better understand modern China

A book by
Stewart Lee Beck and **Sun Zhumin**
Artwork by **Yang Kanzhen**

Shanghai Translation Publishing House

In memory of
**Sima Qian, the Grand Historian
145 – 86 BC**

Portions of this book previously appeared, in different form, on China Simplified and other online platforms.

For more information, please visit www.chinasimplified.com.

also available from China Simplified:
China Simplified: Language Empowerment

Praise for *China Simplified: History Flashback*

"With a splendid combination of wide research and good humour, this book gives readers an excellent introduction to Chinese history from Sima Qian to Chairman Mao. You'll enjoy yourself so much you might not realize how much you're learning. Highly recommended."
— Rana Mitter, Director of the University China Centre, Professor of the History and Politics of Modern China, University of Oxford

"This is the history book for people that didn't know they love history! The authors both entertain and inform with each turn of the page, to leave us with a lighthearted appreciation for the supreme depth of Chinese civilization."
— Yue-Sai Kan, Chinese American television host and producer, entrepreneur, bestselling author and humanitarian

"A delightful romp through 5,000 years of Chinese history. There's something for everybody in this snapshot—vividly illustrated and lucidly explained—of the world's oldest living civilization. Novices to the field will be enlightened; expert Sinologists will be entertained by the witty and often irreverent treatment of a rich history too often obscured by dull prose and pompous exegesis."
— Andrew Browne, China columnist, *The Wall Street Journal*

"This book gives an exciting tour through a long, varied, and fascinating history. Engagingly written and beautifully illustrated, History Flashback *is a wonderful introduction to Chinese culture."
— James Uden, Associate Professor of Classical Studies, Boston University

"Precisely because China is so immense, complex, and contradictory, China Simplified *is valuable in giving a clean, clear line to the main developments in China's history. I found their approach entertaining and enlightening."
— James Fallows, The Atlantic

"A concise yet comprehensive book on Chinese history. It connects Chinese and Western timelines and makes it easy for readers to explore the historic Chinese eras in which they are interested. Those who want to understand China can now do it with ease."
— Jesse Wu, International Vice President, Johnson & Johnson

"As an artist seeking inspiration and further information about my roots in China, China Simplified comes at the perfect time. You cannot improve the future without learning from the past. Stewart and Zhumin have done much of the work pinpointing and distilling details into an easy read!"
— Dana Leong, Grammy Winning Artist, World Economic Forum Young Global Leader

"I admire the authors' passion for Chinese history. This is a delightful adventure in storytelling, and succeeds in making five millenniums of Chinese civilization accessible to readers of all levels."
— James B. Heimowitz, President, China Institute

"Stewart and Zhumin both entertain and inform as storytellers, drawing upon the essential works of Chinese and Western scholars to leave us with an understanding of modern China's many contradictions and challenges."
— Brantley Turner, American Principal, Shanghai Qibao Dwight High School

"As a China consultant for over 40 years, I found this book to be a fun and insightful journey into China's past. I highly recommend it for those who seek to better understand today's China and how it emerged as a global player."
— Greg Whitehorn, Directions Management Consulting

"All multinationals should give China Simplified's books to their executives coming to China for a fun cultural introduction."
— Didi Dai, Tournament Director, IMG Golf, Asia Pacific

"Although highly readable and light-heartedly illustrated, this is a serious book. Whether as an introduction, a refresher, or a deeper dive into the complexities of China, it is highly recommended."
— Harry Harding, University Professor, University of Virginia; Visiting Professor and Senior Advisor to the Institute of Public Policy, Hong Kong University of Science and Technology

"The authors lead us through several thousand years of China's history and conclude (as I did) that the Chinese entrepreneurs of today are an intriguing mixture of modern and ancient: free to innovate, yet held captive to tradition. I hope more people have an opportunity to read this charming and informative book."
— Edward Tse, Founder & CEO, Gao Feng Advisory Company; author of *China's Disruptors: How Alibaba, Xiaomi, Tencent, and Other Companies are Changing the Rules of Business*

"The book's luminous and witty prose takes the reader on a jaunt through the beguiling history of China. This is an ideal gateway to understanding modern China, succinct and vividly expressed."
— George Bobyk, Zhejiang University, MA Chinese History

"This history book is my favorite in the CS series. The illustrations drew me in immediately and I learned many things I didn't know before."
— Al Rocco, China hip-hop performing artist

"An engaging and insightful expedition through China's complex history. I recommended it to anyone interested in a better understanding of modern China through its foundations and the key events of its fascinating past."
— John Cappo, former President and CEO, AEG Asia

"Both informative and fun; a masterstroke!"
— Bruno Lannes, Partner at a well-known consulting company in China

> "For Chinese people, history is our religion ...We don't have a supernatural standard of right and wrong, good and bad, so we view history as the ultimate judge."
>
> — Hu Ping

> "The struggle of humanity against power is the struggle of memory against forgetting."
>
> — Milan Kundera

> "Those who question the present should investigate the past; those who do not understand what is to come should look at what has gone before."
>
> — Guan Zhong

CONTENTS

Why China Simplified?	i
Foreword by Anthony Jackson	v
24 Milestones in Chinese History	vii

ONE — Dawn of the Middle Kingdom — 1
What really happened 5,000 years ago?

TWO — China Catches the Smart Virus — 11
Philosophers who blew everyone's mind

THREE — You *Can* Take It With You — 29
The First Emperor, his Great Wall, and his afterlife army

FOUR — Anyone Here Order a Caravan of Silk? — 45
Han Dynasty intrigues and game-changing inventions

FIVE — Naked in the Woods — 61
Seven Bamboo Sages redefine the meaning of life

SIX — Poets, Prophets, and Pulchritude — 75
Living large in the Tang Dynasty

SEVEN — Why Rule When You Can Be an Artiste? — 93
The Song Dynasty cultural explosion

EIGHT	**What Doesn't Kill You Makes You Stronger** The Mongol conquest of the Chinese heartland	109
NINE	**This Chapter For Mature Audiences Only** Autonomous desires in the Ming Dynasty	119
TEN	**Mind Your Ps and Queues** The Qing Dynasty's potent peaks and quarrelsome quagmires	133
ELEVEN	**Enter the Fashion Icons** Revolutionaries who ignited a nation	151
TWELVE	**Dragon in the Spotlight** Thanks for coming; we've got it from here	171

Resources and References	182
Gratitude	202
About the Authors	203

Why China Simplified?

The journey began with a series of questions we couldn't answer: Why do so many people seem to know so little about China? What is it about China that intrigues us, and captures our imaginations? And, with all that's been written and said about it, why is China still so misperceived and misunderstood? This was the genesis of the China Simplified project.

China Simplified explores and demystifies the country and its people for the rest of the world. By shifting our collective attention beyond the 1% (hot-button issues in the mass media) to the other 99% (relevant conversations about history, language, business, and more), we hope to raise cultural awareness and increase mutual understanding.

Our Quixotic Quest

My twenty-four years living and working among the Chinese has taught me that they are, contrary to popular belief, about the same as people anywhere else. They are normal human beings with similar aspirations. But they bear an ever-present burden of a weighty cultural legacy in an era of stunning change and profound contradictions.

To bring their fascinating story to life, I set out to capture the essence of 5,000 years of Chinese history—the revolutionary ideas of its greatest philosophers, the bold visions of its dauntless leaders, the pivotal events which shaped the modern nation—into one fast-read book for people in a time-starved world. As a non-Chinese, I was certain to elicit a degree of skepticism as I went about my search for the heart of this complex culture. It was as if the legendary Chinese dragon itself stood guard at the gates of culture, eager to incinerate my aspirations. Truth be told, I had doubts of my own. And I've been humbled countless times in the process.

> "It is my ambition to say in ten sentences what others say in a whole book."
>
> — Friedrich Nietzsche

I recruited talented allies in the cause, starting with my longtime production partner, Sun Zhumin, a wonderful storyteller whose husband, Jiang Shaoqing, is an avid Chinese history buff. The problem, in our minds, was not the volume of content. My co-author Zhumin and I have read many epic works in which brilliant authors from both the East and West expound on the mysteries of the Middle Kingdom. Yet here we were, hurtling headlong into the 21st century, awash in alarmist China headline news, subjected to foreign-produced films with superficial Chinese characters, and inundated with political rhetoric, often wildly inaccurate, about the devious plans of those 1.38 billion strangers on the other side of the planet. Is it any wonder why so many of us still don't get China?

Inscrutable people, impenetrable civilization. Westerners are held captive by the myth of an opaque culture. It's what my physics professor referred to as a "don't-know-squared" problem: we don't know what we don't know.

On the Shoulders of Giants

Lü Simian, Liang Shuming, Feng Youlan, John King Fairbank, Tan Qixiang, Chen Kuying, Ezra Vogel, Wang Gungwu, Merle Goldman, Jonathan Spence, Orville Schell, Jonathan Fenby, and Patricia

Buckley Ebrey. These are but a few of the exceptional scholars who've enlightened us with a diversity of historical perspectives and inspired us to persevere with our mission: to forever dispel the fallacy that it's impossible to better understand China and its people. This book seeks not to replace the works of these and other fine writers (see our "Resources" section), but rather to bring their valuable insights into mainstream conversation.

> *"Progress is impossible without change, and those who cannot change their minds cannot change anything."*
>
> — George Bernard Shaw

In any short-form creative work, tradeoffs must be made. Plenty of hours were spent in debate over which historic characters and events to include, and which to omit. Inevitably, some readers will take exception with our decisions, which we hope will stimulate further discussion. We did our best to strike a balance between the ancient and recent past; triumphs and disasters; male and female historical figures; and rich and poor personas. We don't just want to talk about the emperors! And where necessary, we solicited expert guidance in order to select characters and stories which best represent the spirit of their eras. Ultimately, this is a personal work — two persons, passionate about Chinese history, sharing the cultural stories we love most, through our own cross-cultural collaboration.

Zhumin and I hope this book broadens your perspectives and furthers the causes of humanity and diversity.

Stewart Lee Beck
Shanghai, September 2019

Foreword

I've spent much of my career seeking to encourage innovative pathways in education. From my time as Director of the Walt Disney Company's Disney Learning Partnership and work on Capitol Hill with the Select Committee on Children, Youth and Families, to my current role as leader of the Center for Global Education at Asia Society, my consistent goal has been to empower others with a wider, more inclusive worldview.

China Simplified: History Flashback is a highly readable and practical guide to history and culture which embraces this wider worldview. Its authors, Stewart Lee Beck and Sun Zhumin, inspire readers to go beyond stereotyped views of China and its people. Brief yet insightful, this book contains a wealth of stories which capture the zeitgeist of their respective eras, at times contrasted to what was happening elsewhere in the world, in order to provide a profound reflection of the modern Chinese people. After all, in the words of author William Langewiesche, "So much of who we are is where we have been."

> "There is no more pressing issue facing humanity than to nurture a globally competent generation."
>
> — Anthony Jackson

Our lives are being influenced by the reemergence of this once-great power about which the average person seems to know woefully little. I believe that *China Simplified: History Flashback* will find significant appeal among thoughtful business people, students, and travelers alike. It is my hope that this book also finds a home in my own field of education, as an introduction or companion volume to more traditional historic references.

There is an old saying, "Chinese culture belongs to the world." Even beyond the world's oldest living civilization, we have so much of value to learn from each other—East and West, spiritual and secular, developed and developing—as we prepare our youth to engage the world.

We live together on an increasingly interconnected planet. Amidst the daily vicissitudes, and set against the backdrop of long-neglected global priorities, one might conclude that our very survival rests on our ability to cultivate greater empathy for, and discover a new means for constructive engagement with, those most unlike ourselves. And while no single gesture can address a challenge of this magnitude, I applaud the authors and their intentions: to bring the world a little closer together, and in the process, to discover we're actually not that different.

Anthony Jackson
Vice President and Director
Center for Global Education at Asia Society
September 2019

ONE

Dawn of the Middle Kingdom

What really happened 5,000 years ago?

"If there are right men, then the government will prosper; if the right men are lacking, the government will collapse."

— Doctrine of the Mean

A powerful warrior leads his army into battle on an elephant-driven chariot, flanked by dragons, protected below by snakes and shielded above by phoenixes, with other fierce beasts poised to clear the path ahead. Successful in his great quest, the warrior unifies all the tribes of the land and secures the vast Yellow River plain for his people.

Many Chinese consider themselves descendants of that man, the legendary Yellow Emperor (黄帝, *Huáng Dì,* 2697–2597 BC), the first of the five great pre-dynastic rulers. Known as a master of longevity and a prolific inventor, the Yellow Emperor is said to have fathered 25 sons and given 14 of them unique surnames. As a result, genealogists over the ages have tried to trace the ancestries of countless families back to this single ruler, thought to be the progenitor of the entire Chinese race.

This was China's genesis. Unlike peoples who worship an omnipotent creator god, the Chinese revere the Yellow Emperor; Fuxi and Nuwa (China's equivalent to Adam and Eve); the virtuous sage-kings Yao and Shun; and other early humans who've been deified over the ages. These are their mythological superheroes, the initiators of the much-hyped 5,000 years of Chinese history.

Roots of a Civilization

China's dynasties of antiquity—the Xia, Shang and Zhou—spanned eighteen centuries and marked the transition from Neolithic to organized society and recorded time. Historians still debate the existence of the Xia Dynasty (夏朝, *Xià Cháo,* 2070–1600 BC) due to a lack of archeological evidence. Many have written about it, however, including the epic tale of Yu the Great, the tireless founder of the Xia Dynasty. Where previous rulers tried and failed, Yu persevered and halted the massive floods that plagued the Yellow River valley. So passionate was Yu in his work, traveling the lands to dredge the channels that became the rivers of north China, that he passed his own home several times without pause to greet his wife and children. Perhaps many a Tiger Mom has felt the urge to scold her son by saying, "You think ten hours of homework is tough? Imagine being Yu the Great!"

CHINA'S ADAM AND EVE

According to one creation myth, Fuxi (伏羲, Fúxī) and Nuwa (女娲, Nǚwā) were twins, brother and sister, with human heads and snake-like bodies, the only survivors in an ancient land ravaged by a great flood. Fuxi took his sister to the Kunlun Mountain to pray for guidance and ask the heavenly powers about, you know, their bodily urges. Since the earth needed repopulating, the gods sent them a sign to procreate. Perhaps they assuaged their guilt pangs by fantasizing themselves as two complete strangers meeting at the local hot spring.

Shang Dynasty (商朝, *Shāng Cháo,* 1600–1046 BC) kings relied on "oracle bone" divination using pyromancy: Oracles heated up turtle shells and ox scapulae until they cracked. Kings then interpreted the cracks to make major decisions, such as when to attack, where to plant, whom to marry...you get the idea. We know all this because the oracles etched their predictions into the shells, providing us with irrefutable proof of their existence and a window into their minds. What's more, those oracle bone inscriptions evolved over time to become today's Chinese language, the oldest continuous writing system on the planet.

China's Bronze Age commenced around 2000 BC, over a thousand years after those of the Near East and Europe. (That's right, China wasn't first at *everything*.) Advances in bronze technology enabled the Shang kings to make better weapons and perform religious rituals using stunning bronze cauldrons. They sometimes sacrificed humans dozens at a time, to impress deities and ask for favors from their dead ancestors. Those closest to an aging Shang ruler might demonstrate their loyalty by volunteering to accompany him into death. One tomb for a Shang king buried around 1200 BC revealed the remains of 74 humans, 12 horses and 11 dogs, surely not all volunteers. Putting an exclamation point on an era, the final Shang king is most remembered for throwing decadent parties where he floated with concubines in canoes, drank from lakes of wine, and feasted on forests of meat.

China's Good Old Days

Heaven was round, the Earth was square, and benevolent sage-kings cared for the welfare of their people in the Zhou Dynasty (周朝, *Zhōu Cháo,* 1046–256 BC). These were the good old days, according to the master teacher Confucius (more on him in a moment).

The incoming Zhou kings overthrew the Shang in one big bloody battle. They then justified their moral superiority over the corrupt Shang with the "Mandate of Heaven" (天命, *Tiānmìng*), which established that the sacred power of the cosmos would voice its displeasure through famines, floods, earthquakes, or other supreme hardships. This novel concept represented Heaven

EARLY EVIDENCE OF CIVILIZATIONS

CUNEIFORM SCRIPT 3000 BC

Ancient Sumer between Tigris and Euphrates Rivers. Shapes in wet clay chronicled rulers on their monuments. Cuneiform continued until replaced by the Phoenician alphabet after 900 BC.

HIEROGLYPHS 3300 BC

Ancient Egypt along the Nile River. Hieroglyphs were written on papyrus and wood, also etched on temples and monuments, which led to Asiatic alphabets around 1800 BC.

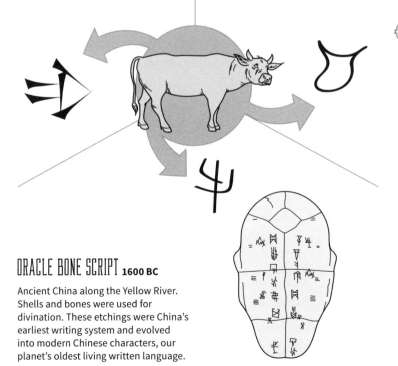

ORACLE BONE SCRIPT 1600 BC

Ancient China along the Yellow River. Shells and bones were used for divination. These etchings were China's earliest writing system and evolved into modern Chinese characters, our planet's oldest living written language.

as an observable set of inclinations, more akin to karma in the Hindu world, rather than the jealous, wrathful God of the Western World. The Chinese emperor has always answered to Heaven, never to the people. Rebellions in China ever since have invoked the Mandate of Heaven in order to usurp power and legitimize claims to the title of rightful ruler, the new "Son of Heaven."

The Zhou maintained most Shang Dynasty customs, but ended slave society and instituted an early form of feudalism in which rulers relied on devoted subjects to cultivate their vast lands and serve as soldiers when called upon. They also reduced the number of sacrifices, and shifted from oracle bone predictions to a divination system using a set of 64 unique hexagram symbols contained in the *I Ching* (易经, *Yìjīng*) Book of Changes.

Recurring events, such as the movement of seasons and the rise and fall of ruling houses, all occurring on one central Yellow River plain for more than 18 centuries, inspired a cyclical rather than a linear view of history. Ethnically diverse neighboring tribes also had an influence, and were eventually seen as potential military allies, an extension of the Zhou culture and its feudal order. This engendered the notion of a "Middle Kingdom" or "Central States" (中国, *Zhōngguó*) as the enduring center of all civilization, still present in China's DNA today.

Children of the Dragon

Western literature depicts dragons as fire-breathing creatures that love to torch villages. So how did the Chinese come to envision a protective, friendly, auspicious symbol of their culture?

Many trace the origins of the Chinese dragon (龙, *lóng*) to the mythical snake-like bodies of Fuxi and Nuwa. The Yellow Emperor furthered its symbolism: His original coat of arms featured a snake. After each conquest, he adopted one potent aspect of the defeated tribe's totem animal. So over time, his snake evolved into something much more complex. If you're on your way home, late at night, and happen to encounter one, you'll recognize the Chinese dragon by its snake-like body, fish-like scales, horse-like mane, mouse-like tail, buck-like horns, cow-like ears, shrimp-like whiskers, and eagle-like claws. But you won't see wings. Chinese dragons fly by magic alone, without the need for aerial appendages.

"LITTLE DRAGON" BRUCE LEE

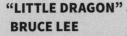

Kungfu master Bruce Lee adopted the stage name *Lǐ Xiǎolóng* 李小龙, (*xiǎolóng* means "little dragon") and wowed audiences to become a Hollywood superstar.

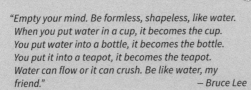

"Empty your mind. Be formless, shapeless, like water. When you put water in a cup, it becomes the cup. You put water into a bottle, it becomes the bottle. You put it into a teapot, it becomes the teapot. Water can flow or it can crush. Be like water, my friend." — Bruce Lee

Unfortunately, China's dragon carries some baggage. As a symbol adopted in the 19th century by China's final dynasty, the Qing, the dragon serves as a reminder of a tragic era when the Chinese suffered at the hands of foreign powers, the so-called Century of Humiliation. As a result, the country is reluctant to reactivate its beloved dragon as a national symbol, for example, on a team uniform or as an Olympic mascot. So the country's elite athletes venture forth dragon-less in pursuit of Olympic gold, and overseas visitors to China's impressive mega-events are greeted at the gate not by friendly dragons, but by insufferably vague cartoon characters that many Chinese can't explain.

Despite these reservations, modern Chinese keep the dragon's spirit alive through celebrations, such as the Dragon Boat Festival. The hit song "Descendants of the Dragon" written by singer Hou Dejian in 1979, and later covered by superstar Wang Leehom, popularized the notion of the Chinese as offspring of a benevolent, mythical creature. In the dragon year of 2012—the dragon being the only imaginary animal among the twelve Chinese zodiac signs—China's auspicious-minded women gave birth to 5% more babies than average. Not to be outdone, Singaporean moms beat the average by 10%.

Couples striving for dragons with early cesarean births, or mothers postponing deliveries beyond the Lunar New Year through sheer willpower, strain the medical system, and eventually, the educational system, when the surge of students competes for limited admissions places. But most consider this a small price to pay for the child's elevated prestige.

DRAGONS: EAST AND WEST

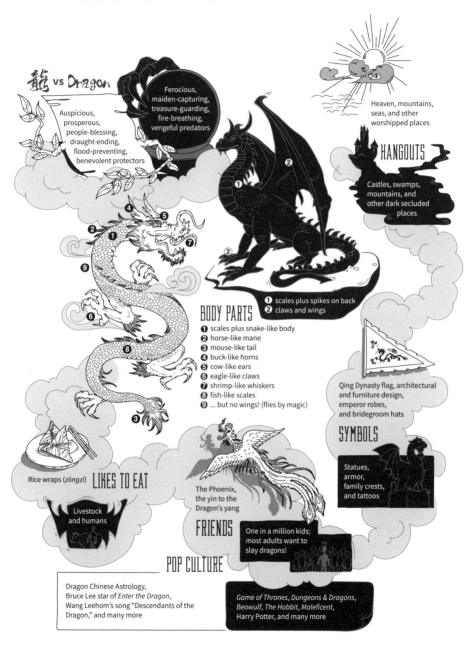

TWO

China Catches the Smart Virus

Philosophers who blew everyone's mind

"How do I know that loving life is not a mistake? How do I know that hating death is not like a lost child forgetting its way home?"

— Zhuangzi

"Philosophy is the highest music."

— Pythagoras

GOLDEN AGE OF CHINESE PHILOSOPHY

Smart guys around the globe in the same era struggled with similar existential issues and often came to similar conclusions.

CHINA | WORLD

Confucius 孔子
551–479 BC

Created a blueprint for restoring the golden age of the sage-kings.

"I am not someone who was born wise. I am someone who loves the ancients and tries to learn from them."

legacy: inspired Confucianism

Socrates
469–399 BC

Used dialectic to examine the meaning of virtue and determine which system is best for the state.

"One thing only do I know and that is I know nothing."

legacy: inspired Western philosophy

Laozi 老子
Sixth century BC

Explored the mysteries of the Dao.

"I have just three things to teach: simplicity, patience, compassion. These three are your greatest treasures."

legacy: inspired Daoism

Buddha
Sixth century BC

Demonstrated the value of detachment.

"Generosity and kind words, conduct for others' welfare, impartiality in all things; These are suitable everywhere."

legacy: inspired Buddhism

Mozi 墨子
470–391 BC

Pioneered early science and challenged Confucian ritual and relationships.

"The business of a benevolent person is to promote what is beneficial to the world and eliminate what is harmful."

legacy: inspired Mohism

Democritus
460–370 BC

Theorized the universe as comprising an infinite number of indivisible atoms.

"Everywhere man blames nature and fate, yet his fate is mostly the echo of his character and passion."

legacy: pioneered modern science

CHINA	WORLD
Zhuangzi 庄子 389–286 BC	**Diogenes** 400–325 BC
Challenged rational thinking to make room for experience and intuition.	Emphasized self-sufficiency and the need for natural, uninhibited behavior.
"No matter how diverse or strange, the Way comprehends them as one."	*"It is not that I am mad, it is only that my head is different from yours."*
legacy: advanced Daoism	legacy: advanced Cynicism
Mengzi 孟子 372–289 BC	**Plato** 429–347 BC
Concluded when bad feelings grow in the heart, they are harmful in governing.	Believed that philosopher-kings who love the sight of truth are alone fit to rule.
"We survive in adversity and perish in ease and comfort."	*"An unexamined life is not worth living."*
legacy: advanced Confucianism	legacy: "Philosophy is Plato, and Plato is Philosopy" — Emerson
Xunzi 荀子 310–235 BC	**Aristotle** 384–321 BC
Believed we are inherently evil and need moral transformation for redemption.	Taught that knowledge is acquired through empirical observation.
"Learning proceeds until death and only then does it stop."	*"Learning is not child's play; we cannot learn without pain."*
legacy: defended Confucianism	legacy: science, metaphysics and more

Kongzi, Laozi, Mozi, Mengzi, Zhuangzi, Xunzi, and Han Feizi. Smart guys for hire. Let's call them the "Zi Crew."

These deep thinkers—the "zi" character in their names means "master"—were among the earliest incubators of a smart virus that circled the globe to inspire the likes of Thales and Pythagoras in Greece, Zarathustra in Persia, and the Seven Rishis in Vedic India. Each set out in different times and places to explore some of life's most important existential questions.

China's Zi Crew personified the Hundred Schools of Thought (诸子百家, *zhūzǐ bǎijiā*) era of fertile intellectual expansion. As the celebrated Zhou Dynasty and its Spring and Autumn period (770–476 BC) deteriorated into the unrelenting violence of the Warring States period (475–221 BC), these philosopher-scholars challenged assumptions and advised feudal lords on how to instill deep loyalty within their court and peaceful order among the masses. As Sinologist Roger T. Ames notes, philosophers traveled from court to court, dispensing wisdom that aimed to lead their patrons to social, political, or military victories. This was a risky job, however. Rulers were often busy and short-tempered, so a single idea could bring the philosopher good fortune, or get him killed.

Ordering the Chaos

Confucius (551–479 BC), whom everyone in China calls *Kǒngzǐ* (孔子) meaning "Master Kong," is the first of our Zi Crew. This idealist yearned for a return to the golden age of benevolent sage-kings, who ruled by divine mandate and observed sacred rituals. Confucius believed coercive regulations were unnecessary; sage-kings could transform society without laws, purely by means of charisma.

Confucius grew up without a father and was raised by his mother. He married early, had a son, then left home and ascended in class to become an advisor to heads of state. His teachings were less about reasoned arguments, like Socrates and the Greeks, and more about how to take proper action to become a person of noble character. As a conduit for Zhou-era wisdom, Confucius shared this refined knowledge to benefit others.

CONFUCIUS
MASTER OF INTEGRITY

"Do not be concerned that no one has heard of you, but rather strive to become a person worthy of being known."

"Those who possess virtue will inevitably have something to say, whereas those who have something to say do not necessarily possess virtue."

"One who knows it is not the equal of one who loves it, and one who loves it is not the equal of one who takes joy in it."

"To make a mistake and yet not change your way, this is called truly making a mistake."

"Someone able to keep past teachings alive and to understand the present is worthy of being a teacher."

"We should look upon the younger generation with awe, because how are we to know that those who come after us will not prove our equals?"

"If you set an example by being correct, who will dare to be incorrect?"

— Confucius

Confucius emphasized the importance of four relationships: ruler and minister, father and son, elder and younger brother, husband and wife. In each of these, the former was expected to protect the latter, and the latter to remain obedient to the former. Bear in mind, this was an age with no legal judiciary where might meant right, and Confucius longed for a peaceful, well-governed land.

Confucianism has been called a religion of common sense, but it's not a religion at all, at least not in a Western sense. It is a stable ordering of society in which people are not equal, yet everyone, especially the ruler, is expected to fulfill their respective roles to the highest standards. The master's values live on today. Even the U.S. Army's slogan, "Be all that you can be," echoes Confucius. He was anti-war, however, and counseled an early version of the Golden Rule: "What you do not wish for yourself, do not impose on others."

We might call these guys the Zi Crew, but their philosophies were quite distinct. Mozi (墨子, *Mòzǐ*, 470–391 BC), a polemic well-versed in the art of philosophical debate, came right after Confucius and undermined all his assumptions. Mozi slammed Confucius' excessive use of rituals, such as elaborate funerals and musical performances, which he said wasted state resources and necessitated tax increases. What's more, Mozi argued, such excess could not possibly end the chaos that plagued society.

Mozi posited that there were three primary hardships on the people: Hunger, cold, and fatigue. His mission was to reduce all three. He urged his followers to go beyond Confucius' limited system of filial relationships, to go beyond compassion for your own group and show concern for all people. In Mozi's mind, this "universal love" or impartial care was the surest means to instill order. Even the Chinese word for "country" (国家, *guójiā*), literally "state family," implies that a single family's happiness is one with that of ten thousand families. Professor He Jinli states, "The great strategy of a peaceful and enduring governing is founded through the law of love."

> *"If something benefits the world, then do it;*
> *if it does not, then stop doing it."*
>
> — Mozi

Mozi wasn't into Confucian self-cultivation either. He pushed for a strict system of rewards and punishments, and advocated direct guidance on all important matters from a strong ruler. (Stay tuned: China will get what Mozi asked for during the upcoming Qin Dynasty.) Mozi believed that the ancient sage-kings cultivated the spiritual power of sacrifices in devotion to ghosts and spirits who would reward the worthy and punish the wicked. For an extra measure of control, the sage-kings also created the Five Punishments: tattooing the face, cutting off the nose, cutting off the feet, castration, and death. A unique brand of philosopher-scholar, Mozi himself maintained the authority to execute his own followers who failed to obey. How's that for tough love?

Like many of the Zi Crew, Mozi was fiercely anti-war. He not only decried the overuse of force by feudal lords of the Warring States, he on more than one occasion rallied his supporters as paramilitary units to defend weaker states against stronger ones. Mozi's philosophy soon fell out of favor with China's warlord rulers and, thanks to ardent Confucius defenders Mengzi and Xunzi, was later swept aside by history in favor of Confucianism.

Mengzi (孟子, *Mèngzǐ*, 372–289 BC), often called Mencius in the West, documented and propagated the spoken teachings of Confucius, who didn't intend to leave any written teachings. Mengzi further attacked Mozi's utopian notion of universal love, arguing that it violates our naturally greater compassion for family members. Mengzi championed a focus on moral education, after the basic needs of food and shelter were met, and posited that a bad environment and the neglect of self-cultivation can destroy one's original (good) nature.

Xunzi (荀子, *Xúnzǐ*, 314–217 BC) was a fellow Confucian who followed in Mengzi's footsteps. However, as a witness to escalating brutality and the downfall of the Zhou Dynasty in 256 BC, Xunzi contradicted Mengzi to argue that human nature is, inherently, bad. He crafted elegant essays to assert that a leader's good example is not enough. Without the external restraint of ritual "neither leader nor follower has hope". Xunzi concluded that our learning process will be slow and difficult—trying-to-unbend-twisted-wood difficult. Xunzi advised, "When you observe goodness in others, inspect yourself, desirous of studying it. When you observe badness in others, examine yourself, fearful of discovering it."

> "Troubled, take care of yourself; successful, take care of the world."
>
> — Mengzi

> "Learning proceeds until death and only then does it stop."
>
> — Xunzi

The eminent modern philosopher Feng Youlan noted that Confucianism arose from certain economic conditions, which themselves were the product of their "Middle Kingdom" geography and mindset. This is why, to the Chinese people, both the system and its theoretical expression were quite natural.

Confucianism would be worshipped and reviled, dissected and debated until the 19th century, when rapid Western industrialization precipitated the end of the Imperial era. China's 20th-century revolutionaries rejected all things Confucian in order to build a new nation, though the existence of nearly 500 Confucius Institutes today worldwide suggests his principles are making a comeback. The master's legacy also lives on in another way: Confucius' father-to-son family tree is now in its 83rd generation, with an estimated two million descendants.

Flowing with the Chaos

Confucius had a contemporary, an elusive free spirit who also longed for a return to an ideal world. This figure attracted a following for his more holistic point of view. Forget the whens, wheres, and hows of his life—historians cannot even decide whether he was a real or composite figure representing life in accordance with the Dao (道, *Dào*, also spelled Tao) meaning "The Way."

The man we call "Laozi" (老子, *Lǎozǐ*), known in the Western world as Lao-Tzu or Lao-Tse, didn't feel the urge to document himself. After all, no true Daoist would ever claim credit for his ideas, let alone pursue fame and fortune. In flow with the underlying natural order of the universe, we connect with our true nature in unselfconscious, effortless action. We also arrive at an understanding that life is essentially meaningless. Not in the sense we don't care about it; rather, we realize that "good or bad" and "right or wrong" exist only as personal judgments.

> *"Sages abide in the business of nonaction,*
> *and practice the teaching that is without words."*
>
> — Laozi

In an era of wicked rulers and shifting borders, Laozi sought refuge in idea of a vast interconnected universe in which man is but a tiny fragment. Daoist landscape ink paintings convey our insignificance, along with a profound wonder at the natural world around us. Laozi would be highly critical of our modern world with its rabid overconsumption and growth-at-any-cost materialism. Laozi's *Daodejing* (道德经, *Dàodéjīng*, lit. "Way Virtue Classic") points to excessive desires as unnatural, and cautions readers that holding onto these desires will lead to a dissatisfying life, and eventually to destitution, want, alienation, and self-destruction. (Sorry Confucius...the worst kind of virtue never stops striving for virtue, and so never achieves it.)

Laozi takes this drama in stride: All force eventually defeats itself and those attempting to impose their will on others will realize the opposite of their intention. And so sages abide in non-doing (无为, *wúwéi*, lit. "do nothing") or noninterference, a state of spontaneous harmony between individual urges and the Way of Heaven. The nonviolent resistance of Mandela, Gandhi, and Martin Luther King is pure Dao, nonaction in action. Do nothing, and yet everything is done (无为而无不为, *wúwéi ér wúbùwéi*). Psychologist Jonathan Schooler cites *wuwei* as an antidote to paralysis by analysis. Once we've achieved a certain degree of proficiency, both at work and in life in general, it's much better to go with the flow.

Of course Laozi wasn't a Daoist and Confucius wasn't a Confucian, just as Jesus wasn't a Christian and Buddha wasn't a Buddhist. Those labels came centuries later, once their original spoken ideas became a system of belief. As time passed, Confucianism borrowed from Daoism, Daoism borrowed from Buddhism and on and on, until many of their stories contained similar messages. A preponderance of evidence suggests most of our world's holy books were edited and revised over time, ostensibly to make the lessons more accessible to the masses. But this also raises the question of how much was lost in translation from language to language and culture to culture over 2,000 years. Borrowing from Mengzi, "One who believes everything in a book would be better off without books." We're back full circle to Laozi's admonition that we are the ones who complicate things.

Zhuangzi (庄子, *Zhuāngzǐ*) was a follower of Laozi who emerged in the same period as the Confucian Mengzi, but the two were poles apart in ideology. Zhuangzi shunned overreliance on thoughts and words, preferring experience and intuition as vehicles for insight. He seemed to take pride in crafting narratives and fictional dialogues that defy understanding.

Here's one of Zhuangzi's more coherent and charming rants: "A trap is for fish: When you've got the fish, you can forget the trap. A snare is for rabbits: When you've got the rabbit, you can forget the snare. Words are for meaning: When you've got the meaning, you can forget the words. Where can I find someone who's forgotten words so I can have a word with him?"

Zhuangzi believed the mystery of life was meant to remain a mystery. Indeed, perfect happiness is the absence of striving for happiness. This unadulterated acceptance of life was echoed many years later by the 20th-century Indian philosopher Jiddu Krishnamurti who shared with followers his secret to life: "I don't mind what happens."

> "Making a point to show
> that a point is not a point
> is not as good as making a nonpoint to show
> that a point is not a point."
>
> — Zhuangzi

David Moser, the Academic Director of CET Beijing Chinese Studies and an avid musician, discovered that Miles Davis' philosophy of jazz seemed to echo centuries of Chinese aesthetics. Davis famously told his sidemen staring with confusion at their music sheets, "Don't play what's there, play what's not there!" Moser reflects, "If that's not Daoism, what is?"

So where is The Way? Zhuangzi said, "There's nowhere it isn't."

Conquering the Chaos

Philosophers weren't the only thought leaders in pre-Imperial Chinese history. The legendary general Sunzi (孙子, *Sūnzǐ*, 544–496 BC), aka Sun Tzu, created a system of military strategy still widely referenced in both the East and West. Sunzi's way of thinking expanded "war" to include all facets of armed struggle, from the strict management of a large army to the crafty execution of the battle plan, and seems to suggest that the ideal general is part Daoist master and part Confucian patriarch.

> "To fight and conquer in all our battles
> is not supreme excellence;
> supreme excellence is causing the enemy
> to submit without fighting."
>
> — Sunzi

Intellectual Chinese may object to the mere suggestion that Sunzi belongs in the same discussion as the revered heavyweights Confucius and Laozi. And perhaps they're right. Indeed, we must look West to appreciate the broader impact of Sunzi's thinking: His *The Art of War* (孙子兵法, *Sūnzǐ Bīngfǎ*) continues to influence more *non-Chinese* leaders—business, political, and military—than any other Zi Crew writing. In Sunzi's day, there were far more military and political treatises in circulation than philosophical or religious ones. University of Pennsylvania Sinologist Victor H. Mair posits that there must have been a large body of military lore attributed to "Master Sun" that spawned a bevy of competing texts. In other words, as a general trying to get hired by a king, you couldn't go wrong by quoting Sunzi in your credentials pitch.

Sunzi's doctrine praises efficient victories. (The clever general not only wins, but wins with ease.) He imposes his will on the opposition while avoiding any imposition of the opposition's will. In the 20th century, Mao Zedong and Ho Chi Minh would bring Sunzi's philosophy full circle, using it to effect victories in China and Vietnam. In the 21st century, military theoreticians view China's rise to power through the lens of Sunzi's strategic thinking. Some modern communication specialists take Sunzi's military tenets one step further, suggesting *The Art of War* is more of a diplomatic playbook, warfare as analogous to persuasion in the battle for hearts and minds. It is a viewpoint espoused by legions of business consultants who draw parallels between Sunzi's philosophies and successful leadership practices.

Perhaps one of the master's better known anecdotes can serve to illustrate: Sunzi served King Helu of Wu, Sunzi's home state. One day, the King decided to challenge his general Sunzi's skills by asking him to train the King's large harem of concubines to become soldiers. Sunzi proceeded to divide the harem into two groups, and selected the King's two favorite concubines as their officers. Sunzi then gave the marching orders. Hearing his first command, all the girls laughed and ignored him, which Sunzi attributed to his own lack of clarity. The girls failed to act on his second command as well, which Sunzi identified as an inability of the two officers to obey and lead. Against the protests of the King, Sunzi executed

SUNZI
MASTER OF STRATEGY

"All warfare is based on deception. Hence, when able to attack, we must seem unable. When using our forces, we must seem inactive. When we are near, we must make the enemy believe we are far away. When far away, we must make him believe we are near."

"When ten times the enemy strength, surround him; when five times, attack him; when double, engage him; when you and the enemy are equally matched, be able to divide him; when you are inferior in numbers, be able to take the defensive; and when you are no match for the enemy, be able to avoid him."

"If you know the enemy and know yourself, you need not fear the result of a hundred battles. If you know yourself but not the enemy, for every victory gained you will also suffer a defeat. If you know neither the enemy nor yourself, you will succumb in every battle."

both girls and appointed two new officers. From then on, the marching was perfect.

As Here so Elsewhere

The Confucians, Mohists, and Daoists all searched for ways to counteract the suffering of their day, not unlike other philosophers around the planet. Author Karen Armstrong writes, "All the sages preached a spirituality of empathy and compassion; they insisted that people must abandon their egotism and greed, their violence and unkindness… You could not confine your benevolence to your own people: your concern must somehow extend to the entire world." Armstrong notes that Socrates himself, sounding eerily Daoist, believed he had a mission to make the Greeks aware that, even when we are most rigorously logical, some aspect of the truth will always evade us.

The Zi Crew's impact on East Asian philosophy was no less profound. Their way of thinking connects us to the core of the Chinese culture, and is almost certain to remain so far into the future. In the words of mythologist Joseph Campbell, "The world is different today…but the inward life of man is exactly the same."

THE DREAM OF ZHUANGZI

The philosopher awoke wondering,
"Am I the one who dreamed of being the butterfly,
or is the butterfly now dreaming of being me?"

THREE

You CAN Take It With You

The First Emperor, his Great Wall, and his afterlife army

*"The sage in governing the people considers
the source of their actions,
never tolerates their wicked desires,
but seeks only for the people's benefit.
Therefore, the penalty he inflicts is not due to
any hatred for the people
but his motive of loving the people."*

— Han Feizi

*"Give me a lever long enough and a prop strong enough,
I can single-handedly move the world."*

— Archimedes

CHINA UNIFICATION TIMELINE
500–200 BC

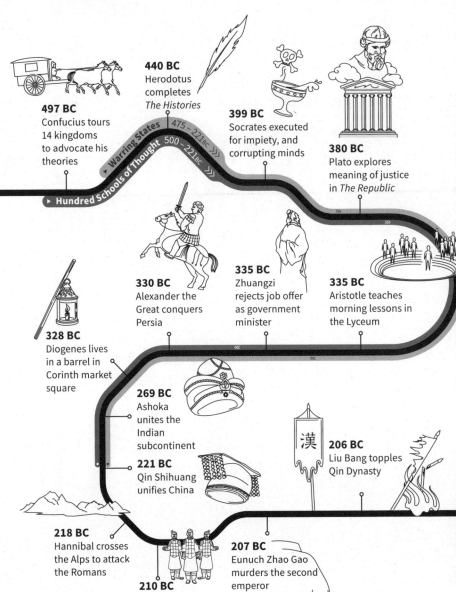

Sorry, but the Great Wall of China is *not* visible from the moon. This popular myth (and tourism-industry boast) was long ago disproved by Neil Armstrong and other carrot-eating astronauts who tried to eyeball it from high earth orbit. What's more, a clever Spanish optometrist named Norberto López-Gil did the math and concluded that identifying the Great Wall from the lunar surface with the naked eye is the ocular equivalent to someone spotting a single human hair from two miles away. Still, there are plenty of other amazing facts about this remarkable work of civil engineering.

Another Brick in the Wall

The Great Wall of China, a two-millennia project, boggles the mind. What started as disconnected stone and packed-earth barriers built by the Warring States (475–221 BC) to protect themselves from northern barbarians and each other became the national obsession during the Qin Dynasty (221–206 BC). Engineers from the Han, Northern Wei, and Ming dynasties later constructed more-formidable walls in the strategic locations of their day. And the bill for this iconic structure, listed among the Seven Wonders of the World? One estimate pegs its total cost at $360 billion in today's dollars, and that's without mentioning the hundreds of thousands of peasants who died building roughly 13,141 miles (21,148 kilometers) of Great Wall. We're talking over $28 million per mile for the defensive centerpiece of several dynasties.

Scholars enjoy debating whether or not the Great Wall achieved its goal of keeping out roaming smugglers, marauding bandits, and evil spirits. The wall and its attendant armies deterred incursions and also served as critical transport and communication routes. On the other hand, invading armies were able to overwhelm or circumvent the system, thus bringing into question the wall's overall effectiveness. For example, the Manchu army gained easy entry in 1644 when General Wu Sangui, a Ming traitor, opened the gates at Shanhai Pass east of Beijing. And the diversion of a million able-bodied men from farming and other vital activities in favor of constructing the wall was a significant drain on the treasury.

Today this monument, built to keep foreigners out, is a major attraction to lure foreigners in. Tourist shops flog colorful tee-shirts proclaiming, "You're not a real man until you've climbed the Great Wall!" (No mention of what laurels await real women who conquer it.) The Great Wall of China captures even our modern imaginations and ranks among our most incredible man-made structures. So let's meet the ambitious leader who set this project in motion.

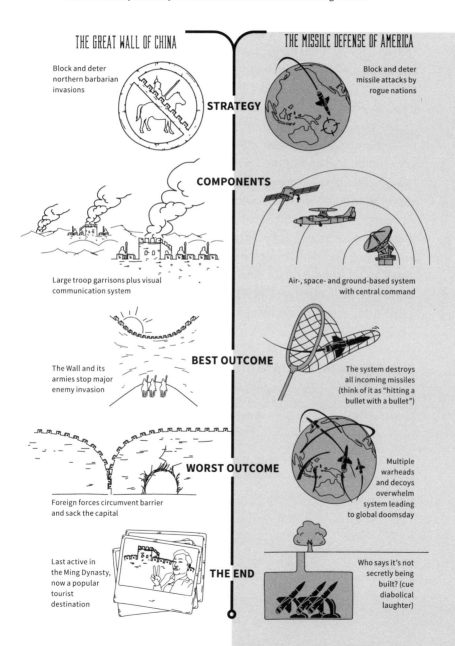

All Work and No Play

Ying Zheng (嬴政, *Yíng Zhèng*, 259–210 BC) came to power as the king of Qin. This westernmost of the Warring States was considered culturally backward during Mozi's time. To the east were the somewhat more refined states of Chu, Wei, Qi, Han, Zhao, and Yan, all battling it out for supremacy, a legacy of the Zhou Dynasty feudalism which first divided the land among the nobles. (Spoiler alert: Ying Zheng will soon kick their noble butts to become China's first emperor.)

Let's back up and put things in perspective. Ying Zheng was but a young man of thirteen when he was crowned king. His great-grandfather had ended the Zhou Dynasty nine years earlier, and the Qin state became the dominant force in the region, despite its lack of sophistication. Iron replaced bronze, and the Qin assembled an advanced fighting force. They had long spears, layered armor, and even crossbows, plus plenty of arable land to feed the army, and a merit system based on how many enemies you kill. Their intent was to conquer their neighbors and wipe out everyone who might later seek revenge. King Zheng took just 26 years to unite all the Warring States under one banner.

CHINA'S WARRING STATES IN 260 BC

After countless battles among hundreds of kingdoms, the western state of Qin emerged as one of the strongest of the main seven states late in the Zhou Dynasty.

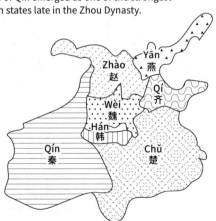

King Zheng ended eight centuries of fragmented rule, and awarded himself the honorary title of Qin Shihuang (秦始皇, *Qín Shǐhuáng*), meaning "the first emperor from the state of Qin" from which the name China originates. But it wasn't all parades and peony petals wafting from the sky. The hard work was just starting.

Imagine yourself as the first Emperor. Your first order of business is to distance your new kingdom from its past. You do that, of course, by knocking down the walls built to separate the states, which prevents the reemergence of their individual powers. You then mobilize a multitude of soldiers, peasants, and slaves to build new walls. That'll keep 'em busy. Don't forget to add watch towers and logistic support networks. And to be extra safe, you melt down all unlicensed weapons and create twelve enormous metal statues for your palaces. So far, so good.

To further protect your rule, your iron-fisted prime minister Li Si burns all the "Hundred Schools of Thought" books and buries the Confucian scholars who might spark dissent. With Confucianism out of the way, supreme allegiance to the state now trumps family loyalties. You threaten to punish all those who fail to report the wrongdoings of their family and neighbors.

It gives you confidence that Li Si is a strong proponent of Han Feizi's doctrine of Legalism, which considers people to be naturally evil, controllable only with plentiful punishments and selective rewards (both trained under Xunzi). You further command Li Si to execute anyone who dares to resurrect old ideas to oppose your new world order. For worse acts of disobedience, say someone who defies your official summons to help build the Wall, you authorize the ancient penalty of *lianzuo*, which results in the death of the guilty party plus his grandparents, parents, uncles and aunts, siblings, children, nieces and nephews, grandchildren, friends, and neighbors. The total body count could number in the thousands.

Did we mention you're showing signs of paranoia? Not to alarm you, but assassins lurk in the shadows.

Your fledgling nation is a mess of incompatible standards. Due to wheel track discrepancies, your subjects cannot even transport basic goods from one end of the country to the other. It's the

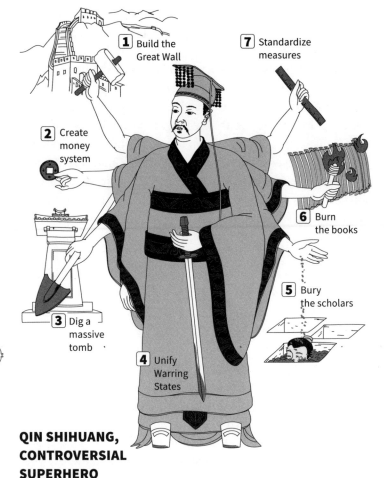

QIN SHIHUANG, CONTROVERSIAL SUPERHERO

equivalent of a train encountering a different rail width every time it crosses a border. So you fix that problem and build an additional 4,250 miles (6,840 kilometers) of new roads. This network is so extensive that the Roman Empire will take several hundred more years to match it. You also mint one common set of coins; unify the written language; expand the legal code; consolidate the weights and measures, and create an administrative system of governance and centralized ruling philosophy still in use today. You do all of this in just eleven years.

Well done, Qin Shihuang! Time for some rest and relaxation. You might be surprised to discover that you are China's only emperor to rule without an empress. Not that you swung the other way. History has it that you sired dozens of children and kept hundreds of "wives" (estimates run from 500–3000 concubines) so don't count on getting too much shuteye.

I'll Sleep When I'm Dead

Qin Shihuang faced a much bigger problem than mortal realm politics. His many failed quests for an elixir of immortality (which likely poisoned him) fueled a fear of what might happen to him when he soon entered the land of the dead. As the afterlife was an accepted fact, families buried the newly deceased with their favorite stuff, anything that might be useful in the next world. The living also feared the sway that the dead held over them, a belief that fostered practices such as ancestor worship and burned

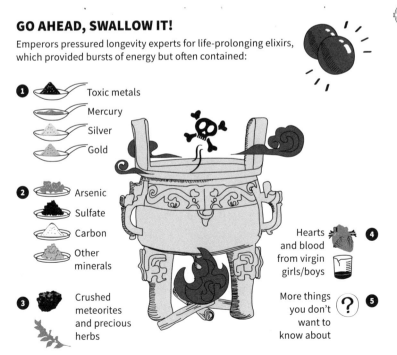

GO AHEAD, SWALLOW IT!

Emperors pressured longevity experts for life-prolonging elixirs, which provided bursts of energy but often contained:

1. Toxic metals
   - Mercury
   - Silver
   - Gold
2. Arsenic
   - Sulfate
   - Carbon
   - Other minerals
3. Crushed meteorites and precious herbs
4. Hearts and blood from virgin girls/boys
5. More things you don't want to know about

offerings to appease disgruntled spirits. In today's China, citizens burn little paper replicas of credit cards, luxury cars, real estate deeds, and digital devices on the *Qingming* (tomb sweeping) spring holiday to show affection for their deceased loved ones.

Qin Shihuang demanded a massive army of terracotta warriors able to vanquish all those he had already killed, now waiting to seek revenge in the spirit world. The stone army would of course necessitate a miniature version of his entire empire, complete with flowing rivers of poisonous mercury and booby traps to dispatch any tomb raiders who dared encroach on his underground kingdom. A select group of concubines and servants were honored with the opportunity to make final preparations inside his tomb until — oops — the doors were closed behind them.

> *"I am Emperor. My descendants will be numerous. From the second generation to the ten thousandth, my line will not end."*
>
> — Qin Shihuang

Farmers outside the modern city of Xi'an discovered the terracotta warriors' tomb in 1974 while digging a well. (As of this writing, one of those farmers still greets tourists and autographs books outside the museum.) Although the burial location of Qin Shihuang was well-documented, archeologists arriving on the scene had no idea they were about to spend the next five years excavating three massive pits spanning 22 square miles (56 square kilometers) in which 8,000 stone warriors awaited them. The terracotta warriors have since welcomed over 70 million visitors. After paying your entrance fee to gaze upon this incredible stone army, you may be shocked to learn that the nearby tomb of Qin Shihuang itself has yet to be unearthed. Its sublime contents remain a mystery, despite the public clamor to find out what's inside. Authorities prefer to wait, decades more or longer if they must, for the arrival of enhanced technologies to ensure the rare treasures sealed within will survive the excavation process.

THE TERRACOTTA WARRIORS

Qin Shihuang's soldiers were all individually painted in color. Unfortunately, the paint oxidized after the tombs were opened.

Foot Soldiers
Majority of stone warriors are like them; weapons lost or deteriorated

Archers
Standing lower ranks surround kneeling higher ranks

Cart Drivers
Arms out to hold reigns of horse

Mobile Soldiers
No, they're not practicing dance moves; their hands are resting on a cart

Cavalry
Shorter skirts for easy horse riding

Officer
His hat and scarf reveal his rank

General
Elaborate full-body armour and headgear

The First Emperor made a glorious entrance into the afterworld, but his above-ground handover of power was a monumental disaster. He had intended his oldest son, Fusu, to succeed him as second emperor. He even declared it in his will. The court eunuch Zhao Gao and his co-conspirators feared that the strong-willed Fusu would banish them from the palace when he returned from battle. So before they announced the first emperor's death, they created a bogus will declaring his more easily-manipulated youngest son, Huhai, as the new emperor. A bloodbath ensued, leaving all the rightful heirs dead. The Qin Dynasty collapsed four years later.

WHOSE CRYPT IS MORE FAMOUS?

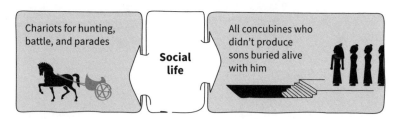

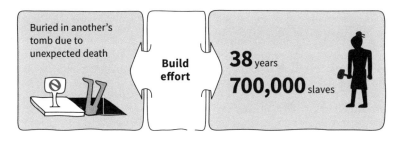

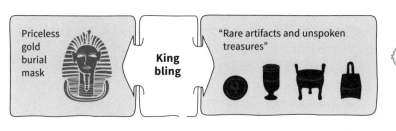
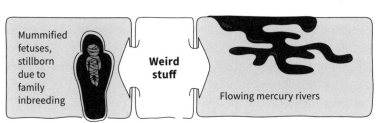
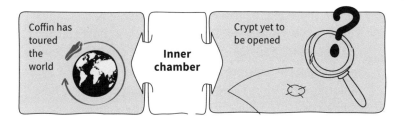

Battle of the Blood Brothers

After the fall of the Qin Dynasty, warlord leaders Xiang Yu of the Chu state and Liu Bang of the Han battled for five years, leaving a legacy replete with cunning, deception and intrigue.

Xiang Yu the Conqueror (项羽, *Xiàng Yǔ*, 232–202 BC) was the Napoleon of his time, a charismatic leader in total command of an unbeatable army. On multiple occasions, Xiang Yu allowed the treacherous bandit Liu Bang (刘邦, *Liú Bāng*, 256–195 BC) to escape, believing himself far superior. In one such escape, Liu Bang is said to have pushed his own children off a chariot to make it go faster! After capturing Liu Bang's father, Xiang Yu tried to force Liu Bang's surrender by threatening to cook his father. Liu Bang knew Xiang Yu considered him a blood brother of sorts, after all, they fought side by side as allied rebels against the Qin. He also recognized Xiang Yu's nice-guy Achilles heel. So he responded: "My father is your father, so go ahead, I'll share the soup with you."

Chen Kaige's epic film *Farewell My Concubine* dramatized the tale of Xiang Yu's concubine, Yu Ji, who killed herself to avoid being a distraction. A touching gesture, but all in vain. Liu Bang's victory launched the Han Dynasty — he became its first emperor, with the honorary name Han Gaozu, while Xiang Yu's emotional defeat inspired a slew of TV dramas.

In its 422-year history, the Han Dynasty would be led by 29 emperors, all descendants of the Liu family. So you might wonder, why didn't they just call it the "Liu Dynasty"? Because its founder, Liu Bang, came from the Han state and he chose that name instead. This practice is similar to European nomenclature: Each of France's 19 King Louis's abandoned his birth name in order to accord with tradition. In so doing, Liu Bang set a naming convention adopted by all future dynasties, as well as an identifying label for the Chinese race. "The name of the Han ethnic group originated after Liu Bang established the dynasty," notes acclaimed historian Lü Simian. The Han ethnicity now constitutes 92% of modern China's people, though centuries of intermarriage among the East Asian races have created a much more dynamic human melting pot than this number might suggest.

CHINESE CHESS

Mythology credits the ancient tribal leader, Shun, with the creation of Chinese Chess (中国象棋, *zhōngguó xiàngqí*). The middle section dividing the board later became known as the "River Chu" and "Border Han," indicating the two armies which clashed after the fall of the Qin Dynasty.

Similar to Western Chess (国际象棋, *guójì xiàngqí*), the object is to capture one piece, the General. Soldiers, horses, and chariots move like pawns, knights, and rooks, however, cannons capture by jumping, and, like the game Go (围棋, *Wéiqí*), pieces move between the points of intersecting lines.

Surprise, surprise: It's the most-played board game in the world.

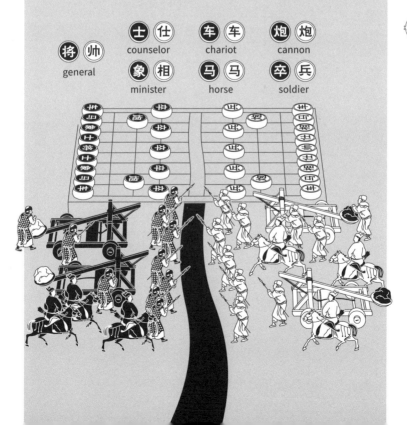

Anyone Here Order a Caravan of Silk?

Han Dynasty intrigues and game-changing inventions

"When the fast rabbits are caught,
the hunting dogs are killed for meat.
When the enemy empire is destroyed,
the generals are executed."

— Han Xin

"Without the invention of stirrups in China,
feudalism would be non-existent in Europe."

— Joseph Needham

HAN AND ROMAN ERA TIMELINE

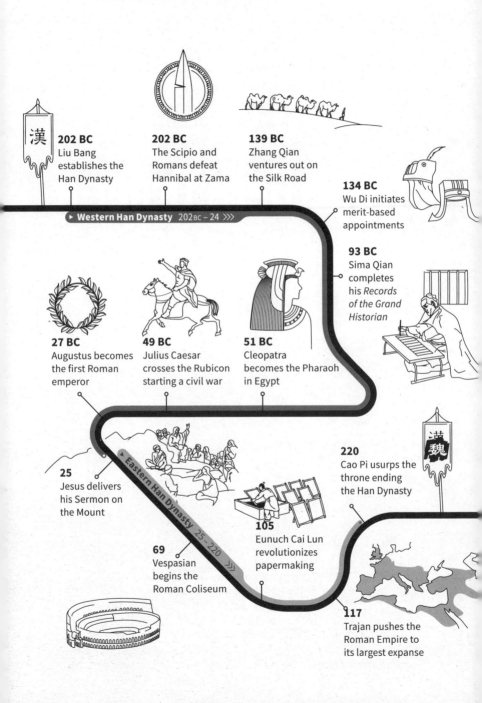

At the start of the Han Dynasty (202 BC – 220 AD), the West knew little of China's existence. That was soon to change, as the dynasty initiated an unprecedented era of innovation, trade, and ideas.

Imagine the wonderment on the faces of Roman court officials when they first touched a piece of luxurious silk. Its lightness, luminosity, and strength must have seemed otherworldly. The production methods of this legendary fabric were once a closely-guarded Chinese state secret whose divulgence was met with unspeakable punishments, far worse than if you busted into the safe in Atlanta and stole the formula for Classic Coke.

Silk's origins two thousand years earlier are shrouded in mystery. A Chinese folk tale holds that Lei Zu, wife of the legendary Yellow Emperor, was sipping tea under a mulberry tree when a silk cocoon fell from the tree, plopped into her cup, and unraveled into super fine thread. Seized by inspiration, Lei Zu collected several of these peculiar cocoons and wound the fine thread into thicker threads suitable for producing garments. The rest is history.

Much later, when the raw materials and the know-how of silk were smuggled out of China—some say by a Chinese princess who hid silkworm eggs and mulberry seeds in her headdress when she left to marry a Khotan king in the west; others say by two unscrupulous monks who hid them in their canes—it would have been one of our world's first major intellectual property thefts. As silk's popularity grew, so did its notoriety. Muslim scripture forbid men from wearing it. Roman philosopher Seneca the Younger proclaimed: "I can imagine clothes made of silk, if materials that do not hide the body, nor even one's decency, can be described as clothes."

The First Journey to the West

The Silk Road spans 4,350 miles (7,000 kilometers) over rugged terrain linking China with the Middle East, India, and Europe. A portion of this vast network of trails originated as a means for armies to carry home captured loot. And when the first Han Chinese expedition party ventured west out of the Han capital of Chang'an (now called Xi'an), into one of the harshest stretches of

THE MYSTERY OF SILK

Collect Eggs
Each female moth lays 200–300 eggs onto paper or cloth sheets.

Hatch and Feed
Baby silkworms hatch from the eggs and eat mulberry leaves. Traditionally, the first hatching comes three days after the Tomb Sweeping Day in early April.

Test Readiness
Check between the silkworm's rear pair of legs—if you see a gray mass, it's too early; when the mass turns translucent, the silkworm is ready to cocoon.

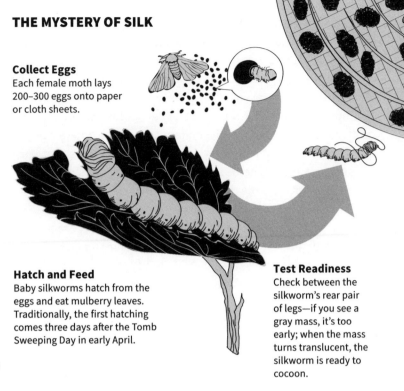

the Silk Road, they were not overloaded with bolts of silk and eager to barter. They were in search of regional allies to gang up against China's troublesome northwest neighbors, the Xiongnu.

Zhang Qian (张骞, *Zhāng Qiān*, 164–113 BC), an early Han diplomat later dubbed the "Father of the Silk Road," led this fated expedition in 139 BC. Not far into their journey, they were captured by the Xiongnu. After a year of captivity, they escaped and continued westward through the desert. On their way back to China, wouldn't you know it, the Xiongnu captured them again. All told, Zhang Qian's gallant crew were gone for 13 long years. No wonder they returned to Chang'an with a collection of amazing stories, plus a wealth of insights that changed the emperor's strategic thinking.

In the centuries ahead, the elite families of Chinese, Turks, and Mongols intermarried to build trust and encourage regional stability. Beyond precious goods and raw commodities, the

Warm Silkworms
Move the silkworms into bamboo trays kept warm by a low flame. They become comfortable and secrete fast-drying liquid silk to spin cocoons.

Collect Cocoons
Silkworms seal themselves inside a cocoon in just two days. The entire process, from egg to complete cocoon, takes 20–25 days.

Extract Thread
Cocoons are softened in boiling water. Workers locate the end of the thread and unwind the cocoon to 1–1.5 kilometers of continuous thread.

Prep For Sale
Dyeing, weaving, and spinning

Silk Road would facilitate an exchange of creativity, art, and religion. We might say that it was our world's first information superhighway.

The Golden Age of the Han

Han Wudi (汉武帝, *Hàn Wǔdì*, 156–87 BC) was the fifth emperor of the Western Han Dynasty and its most prolific. His 54-year reign, one of China's three longest, was filled with impressive accomplishments.

After Qin Shihuang unified China's territories, Wudi unified its ideology and established Confucianism as a stabilizing force and dominant school of thought for 2,000 years. He even managed to sneak out of the capital in disguise to go hunting and have some fun.

SILK ROAD: HANS AND ROMANS COMPARISON

German geographer Ferdinand von Richthofen dreamed up the name "Silk Road" in 1877, captivated by the storied history of the trade route connecting China, India, Persia, Arabia, Greece, and Rome by land and sea.

Commodities flowing West to East:
High quality glass, gems, rugs, fabrics, gold embroidery, exotic fruits, and animals.

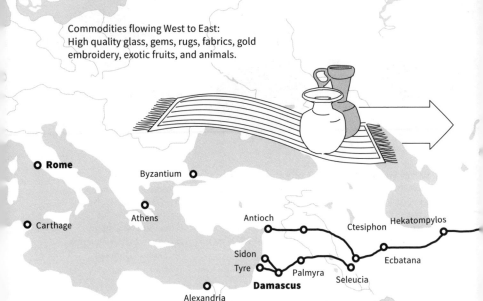

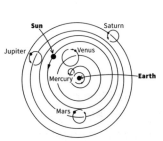

Ptolemy theorized in 150 that the Earth was stationary and at the center of the universe.

Stola was one of the proper garments for married women, usually hanging from the shoulders with short straps, draping over an undergarment.

The Pantheon was rebuilt and completed in 125. Arched vaults and granite columns were most pervasive in Roman architecture.

Commodities flowing East to West:
Silk, porcelain, jade, bronze ornaments, medicines, paper, tea, and spices.

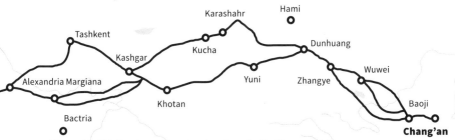

Life on the Silk Road was a spectacular struggle. Each caravan of precious goods required a small army to frighten away roving bandits. Relations between the Han Dynasty and the Roman Empire were mostly indirect, with the Parthians, Kushans, and others serving as intermediaries.

The Imperial Ancestral Temple of West Han was built in 150 BC. Wooden columns and beam-supported roofs were common structures in Han architecture.

Quju a full body garment, was popular among women. Fabric wrapped under the arms to the back, leaving an open collar.

Zhang Heng suggested in 120 that the universe was like an egg, with stars on the shell and the Earth as the central yolk.

Wudi made all the right moves in terms of governance. In the aftermath of the super-intense Qin Dynasty, he relaxed the demands on the people for forced labor and carried on the "ruling by not ruling" philosophy of Han founder Liu Bang. Wudi also neutralized the Xiongnu threat along the border and doubled the size of China through successive conquests. This expansion would exceed the maximum footprint of the Western Roman Empire established 200 years later by the prolific soldier-emperor Trajan.

But Wudi faced his fair share of challenges. To pay for his escalating military costs, he raised taxes, nationalized private businesses, and confiscated property of the nobility, which also eliminated them as potential adversaries. Meanwhile, the number of peasant revolts had increased. Wudi ordered his officials to suppress rebellion in their regions or face execution. So most officials covered up their problems and told Wudi what he wanted to hear. Wudi's home life was no less problematic. Eunuchs spread misinformation around his court. His many wives, concubines, and kids vied for his attention, while mother-in-laws and entire family clans maneuvered against each other for hereditary dominance. In the end, nobody could agree on who to bury with him!

"Since I became emperor, I've done wrongs and worried my people. How regretful am I."

— Han Wudi

According to legend, Wudi coveted a tomb befitting his mighty reign. Size counts, but when it comes to tombs, it's location, location, location — where you rest and what you overlook. So in the second year of his reign, Wudi commissioned his top feng shui master to pinpoint the most auspicious final resting place, which was believed to further ensure his dynasty's continued prosperity. Sure enough, the feng shui master found the perfect plot, a truly once-in-an-eternity location, where one could gaze upon the most exquisite scenery fully reclined on the hillside. Temptation

THE FOUR GREAT INVENTIONS

English scientist and philosopher Francis Bacon wrote that Chinese printing, gunpowder, and the compass altered the state of the world.

Gunpowder
This volatile substance, a 9th century lucky mistake in the quest for longevity, resulted in better fireworks (and okay, more efficient warfare). Due to careless handling in 1280, a massive gunpowder warehouse exploded and sent body parts on an unplanned holiday into the next county.

Compass
A concept first discussed during the Han Dynasty and perfected in the Song, it facilitated an era of worldwide exploration and discovery (plus way fewer shipwrecks).

Printing
Ideally suited for Chinese characters, woodblock printing on textiles began in the late Han, while printing on paper for mass communication took off during the Tang.

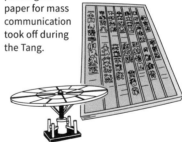

Paper
Han eunuch Cai Lun mixed a mishmash of plant fibers, fishnet, old rags, and hemp waste to create paper. It was originally used to wrap things, rather than capture profound thoughts. Soon people were writing love notes and sharing dumb ideas. Woohoo!

The Four Great Inventions (四大发明, Sì Dà Fāmíng) were created for domestic use—their value in trade was more of an afterthought—as China still saw itself as the center of civilization. China also designed people-focused inventions such as the plow, wheelbarrow, horse collars and stirrups, silk loom, matches, kites, parachutes, and hot air balloons.

proved too great, however. To his esteemed emperor, the feng shui master presented a plot where you still had to sit up to enjoy the beautiful vista. The sneaky feng shui master kept the best location for himself!

Despite his shortcomings, Wudi is still considered the best of the Han emperors and among the greatest in China's history. What's more, he was one of the few self-reflective emperors who openly acknowledged his mistakes in order that he might better rule in his remaining years and benefit future emperors. Under Wudi's leadership, the Han Dynasty enjoyed an extended period of prosperity and established Confucian values across a diverse Chinese society.

No doubt Confucius, Mengzi, and Xunzi are smiling in their tombs.

The Heroic Historian

To record the many examples of his greatness, Emperor Wudi appointed Sima Qian (司马迁, *Sīmǎ Qiān*, 145–86 BC) as his Grand Historian. A well-traveled student of Confucian tradition, Sima Qian cherished the role of documenting the Chinese civilization dating back thousands of years. Scholars often compare him to the Greek historian Herodotus, whom the Roman orator Cicero called the "Father of History." Sima Qian wanted to bring truth and accuracy to the art of recordkeeping. After all, this was his one moment of glory, the chance to etch his name in the annals of history by way of recording the heroic deeds of others. In real life, of course, it doesn't always work out that way.

Wudi took exception to Sima Qian's portrayals of his actions, which weren't nearly godlike enough for his tastes. What's more, Sima Qian insinuated that Wudi was running a Legalist (brutal) rather than a Confucian (refined) government. So when friction arose and Sima Qian defended a military officer whom Wudi blamed for a defeat by the Xiongnu, Wudi sentenced Sima Qian to death. To avoid execution, Sima Qian was given a choice: buy his way out of trouble (who has that kind of money?) or suffer castration. Some choice, huh?

EUNUCH SURGERY, THE GRUESOME TRUTH

How eunuchs become eunuchs, from the recollections of Qing Dynasty eunuchs (Warning: this section not for the squeamish!)

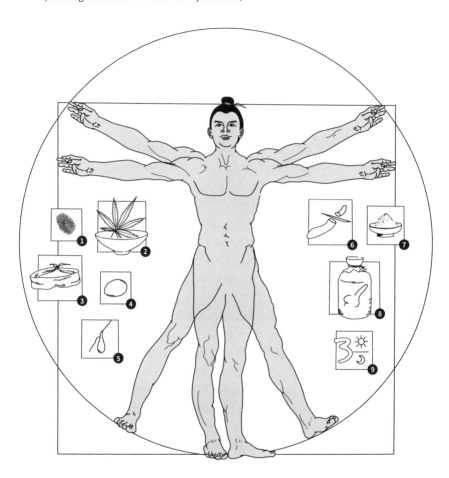

❶ Sign agreement to waive the castrator of any liability ❷ Drink marijuana water while they clean your private parts ❸ Lie on bed with all four limbs and waist tightly tied, eyes covered ❹ Hard-boiled eggs are stuffed in your mouth to prevent screaming ❺ Deep cut to your ball sack to squeeze out testicles, cuts covered with pig bile to stop the bleeding ❻ Slice off your penis, a high-skill operation: if they cut too shallow, you'll need more surgery, if they cut too deep, you'll pee uncontrollably ❼ Penis and testicles dried in lime powder and stored atop the main beam in castration house for good luck in your career ❽ If you become rich one day, you can buy back your body parts later at a price decided by the castrator; that way you can be buried complete ❾ It takes three days for you to recover; they say day three is the worst

> "When I have truly completed this work, I shall store it at the famous hideaway mountain until it may be handed down to men who will appreciate it so that it may reach the great cities of the world. That way my time lost to this humiliation will be worth it, and even if there were worse sufferings, what regret shall I have?"
>
> — Sima Qian

After the cruelest cut, Sima Qian persevered through three years of imprisonment, driven by the need to finish his masterwork, *Records of the Grand Historian* (史记, *Shǐjì*). His lively narrative features active discourse to show how historic outcomes were the result of human decisions. It even introduces the narrator himself as a character. This landmark document, over half a million characters long, was the first of China's 24 official historic records (earlier historic records were shuffled aside), still revered to this day for its reliability and balance. Sima Qian died eight years later, a heroic historian.

Later during the Han Dynasty, in the year 25 AD, castration became compulsory for all men living in the imperial palace. Eunuchs served a special role — they woke the emperor in the morning, attended to his many needs all day, and delivered concubines to him at night. And unlike powerful generals and plotting officials, eunuchs were unable to create descendants and thus harbored no secret plans to seize power and start their own dynasty. To an emperor, they were safe allies, even if they peddled influence and manipulated the system.

Eunuchs as trusted advisors and harem protectors was nothing new (the Sumerians did it thousands of years earlier), although the exact definition of a eunuch varied by, ah, which bits get chopped off. In Han China, it meant losing the pork and the beans. But there was never a shortage of parents willing to commit their precious sons to this corporeal sacrifice in order to elevate their family's wealth and prestige. By the end of the Ming Dynasty in 1644, historians estimate there were over 100,000 eunuchs in countrywide service to the emperor.

AUTOBIOGRAPHY OF AN EMPEROR

Nearly the same story occurred again and again in Chinese imperial history.

Act 1:
Mission Impossible

1. Mom becomes concubine with really good skills of persuasion.
2. Mom gives birth to a son (me!) and becomes emperor's favorite.
3. The "men without thingees" all love me and mom.
4. Mom becomes empress; Dad's mom (empress dowager) not happy.
5. Dad dies and I become Son of Heaven. Yippee!!! Sorry, Dad.

Act 2:
Let The Good Times Roll

1. Mercilessly crush my opponents. This is fun!
2. Audition first thousand concubines; names hard to remember.
3. Mom always telling me what to do; sick of her always being right.
4. Dad's mom accidentally hangs herself; that frees up a bedroom.
5. Running China is hard! Note to self: hire more men without thingees.
6. Celebrate my 15th birthday! Why does Mom hate my hottest wives?
7. I am a great father who loves all his sons. Oh, the daughters too.
8. Mom marries off daughters with barbarians to mix our blood lines.
9. Men without thingees help me choose a successor, just in case.

Act 3:
Who Wants To Live Forever

1. Men without thingees can't agree on anything. Who needs this stress?
2. We're broke?! Raise taxes and execute those who grumble!
3. I demand more concubines and pursue life of leisure.
4. Man without a thingee gives me secret elixir of immortality—woohoo!
5. Wake up dead, WTF?! Note to self: ask about elixir, delayed reaction?
6. This tomb is awesome, thanks Mom!!!

Romance of the Three Kingdoms

"The long divided must unite, the long united must divide; thus it has ever been." This prophetic opening line of *Romance of the Three Kingdoms* (三国演义, *Sānguó Yǎnyì*) by Luo Guanzhong, one of China's Four Great Novels. It mixes history and legend to dramatize the bloody and turbulent Han to Jin Dynasty transition from 169 to 280. With each new emperor, society once again marks time from zero in a new era of triumphs and disasters, further reinforcing the cyclical Chinese view of history.

A Hollywood producer might pitch this mega-novel, containing nearly a thousand unique human characters, as "Ken Burns meets *Game of Thrones*." Luo Guanzhong's widely read story collection portrays the intrigues and struggles of the Wei, Shu, and Wu family states (aka the Three Kingdoms), often drawing comparisons with Shakespeare's entire catalog.

Modern Chinese recall its most famous characters with fondness, including the reluctant military advisor, Zhuge Liang, (诸葛亮, *Zhūgě Liàng*, 181–234) who helped the Southern army defeat a much more powerful Northern army. At the battle of Red Cliff, in which the outmanned South seemed doomed to defeat, Zhuge Liang devised the strategy of attacking the enemy as they crossed a river, exploiting their weakness. Another time, upon discovering that a superior army led by Sima Yi was marching towards Xi Cheng, its destruction a near certainty, Zhuge Liang advised opening the main gate and leaving the town unprotected. When the invaders arrived, Sima Yi saw the open gate and, fearing a trap, ordered an immediate retreat. By virtue of these classic tales, Zhuge Liang was glorified because he tipped the balance of the war despite having no formal military training.

After six decades of real-life battles for the throne in China, it became nearly impossible for any aspiring official to guess which ruling clique might be here today and gone tomorrow. The time was ripe for an intellectual challenge to the unquestioned advantage of becoming a government official.

Naked in the Woods

Seven Bamboo Sages redefine the meaning of life

*"If the Way is being realized in the world, then show yourself;
if it is not, then go into reclusion."*

— Confucius

"No one is free, even the birds are chained to the sky."

— Bob Dylan

There were hippies in China over 1700 years ago. We're talking freedom-loving hedonists who wanted to escape from restrictive Confucian officialdom during the brief Three Kingdoms (220–280) period. Daoism, with its connection to nature, was a much better fit for this lot, and provided a framework beyond their worldly frustrations.

The Seven Sages of the Bamboo Grove (竹林七贤, *Zhúlín Qīxián*) were a group of writers, musicians, and scholars from multiple generations, teenagers up to forty-somethings, so named because they took pleasure in alcohol-fueled philosophical debates and poetic expression secluded in the bamboo forests of northwest Henan. Insiders turned outsiders, they represented Epicurean liberation during a post-Han era of power battles, conspiracy theories, and multiple *coups d'état*. Their eccentric, indulgent conduct was less "Fight the Power" civil disobedience and "Give Peace A Chance" idealism than it was pragmatic avoidance of dangerous political entanglements. As the old saying goes, "Being close to the emperor is like being close to a tiger."

None But Ourselves Can Free Our Minds

Ji Kang (嵇康, *Jī Kāng*, 223–262) was the spiritual ringleader of the Seven Sages. Articulate and multitalented, he was a master of the *gǔqín* (古琴), a plucked seven-string instrument often associated with Confucian scholarly refinement. In many ways, Ji Kang was the quintessential Daoist who preferred to compose music and explore philosophy rather than get caught up in the rat race. Ji Kang's impressive rhetoric and poetry swayed the minds of many, until government officials made clear their intent to lure this reprobate back into their ranks.

> "A man without ideals is not a man."
>
> — Ji Kang

Ruan Ji (阮籍, *Ruǎn Jí*, 210–263), a son of a famous scholar and a recognized poet in his own right, developed an uncanny ability to avoid aristocratic obligations by cultivating the image of a drunken madman. When confronted by a ruling family's demands for his daughter's hand in marriage, Ruan Ji remained drunk for two months until the family gave up attempting to communicate with him. Some historians recount a more serious side of Ruan Ji, a man who would shut himself away for days on end to read the classic philosophers, in search of insight and truth in what he saw as an imperfect world.

Ruan Ji is also known for poetry about the love of men during a period known for its homosexual openness. Most of the Sages had wives and kids, and side dalliances were not an uncommon occurrence. Histories note the prevalence of imperial court "favorites" during several dynasties, with the art of flattery leading to positions as favored officials, sometimes justified as being part of the larger natural order. Another common poetic allusion in the literature of the times is the enjoyment of "clouds and rain," which, rather than a weather forecast, refers to the act of lovemaking.

> *"Surely you do not mean to suggest that*
> *the rules of propriety apply to me."*
>
> — Ruan Ji

The older and more responsible Shan Tao (山涛, *Shān Tāo*, 205–283) bounced back and forth between the Bamboo Grove and officialdom to pursue career ambitions. Ji Kang detested Shan Tao's overly pragmatic behavior, since Shan Tao was the one who united the Sages as refugees of the system. Shan Tao's wife, Lady Han, once queried her husband about his close relationship with Ji Kang and Ruan Ji. Shan Tao explained that they're the only people with whom he wanted to be friends. Still curious, she secured his permission to spy on the other men that night. Returning to her bedroom at dawn, Lady Han confided to her husband that she had peeped through a hole drilled in the wall to observe Ji Kang and

Ruan Ji. She noted their powerful connection and physical prowess, declaring that Shan Tao was their equal in intellect alone. Watching the clouds and rain? You naughty girl.

The big drinker of the group, Liu Ling (刘伶, *Líu Líng*, 221–300), was less intellectual but lightened the mood with his penchant for singing poetry and stumbling around naked. When puzzled guests inquired about this odd habit, Liu Ling responded, "Heaven and Earth are my home, and my house is my pants, so what are you all doing here between my legs?"

SAGES AND HIPPIES
A spiritual connection across the ages?

The Seven Sages were countercultural intellectuals who practiced Daoism in a bamboo forest to escape roles in the heavy-handed Confucian government of their time.

The Hippies were countercultural idealists in search of a better tomorrow, who rejected industrialized mainstream values and protested the U.S.-led war in Vietnam.

1. Born out of chaos

Country fractures following Han Dynasty. Wei/Jin era frequent coups d'etat.

Vietnam War protests. Assassinations of Kennedy brothers and Martin Luther King.

2. Hub of origin

Bamboo grove in Northwest Henan

Bohemian neighborhoods of San Francisco, California

3. Chemical prompter

Wushisan — A stone powder made from fluorine, quartz, red bole clay, stalactite, and sulfur. Its psychedelic and heating effects are said to prompt eccentric behavior and make one wax poetic.

LSD — Lysergic acid diethylamide's mind-altering and hallucinogenic effects are said to create visual, sensory, and spiritual experiences that awaken us to our true nature.

4. Sing along with

Ruan Xian, plucked string instrument with 4 strings over 24 frets

Guitar, plucked string instrument with 6 strings over 22 or 24 frets

Liu Ling also enjoyed riding in a deer-drawn carriage, jug of grain wine in hand, like some kind of bad Santa slurring *"Hao hao hao!"* (Good good good!) instead of "Ho ho ho!" To his entourage he instructed, "If I drink myself to death, you guys bury me," and to his wife, "When I die, bury me with wine fermenting over my head."

By now you might be wondering, what were these dudes tripping on? *Wushisan* (五石散, *wǔshísǎn*, lit. "five-stone infusion") is a man-made medical powder invented by renowned Han physician Zhang Zhongjing to treat typhoid. The Sages weren't feeling unwell, only chasing *Wushisan's* peculiar side effects: profuse sweating, tender skin, hallucinations, and an added benefit closely resembling something you'd get these days from a little blue pill. Goes a long way to explaining why they spent the bulk of their days chilling in a bamboo forest and drinking themselves silly.

So Much For Wanting To Be Left Alone

Ji Kang didn't do himself any favors by refusing invitations to rejoin the government. Soon he faced a charge of "perversion of public morals," or, in more common parlance, treason. To shelter Ji Kang from certain death, Shan Tao even offered his own official position to Ji Kang. Three thousand students from the Imperial College gathered at the site of his beheading to request Ji Kang as their teacher and a waiver of the severe penalty, a gesture of respect and admiration that the Jin emperor rejected.

THE MAGIC OF BAMBOO

zhú

Bamboo Facts

- A member of the grass family, bamboo originated in ancient China over 5,000 years ago.

- Over 1,500 species located on every continent except Europe and Antarctica.

- According to Guinness World Records, certain species of bamboo can grow 3 feet (91 cm) in a single day!

Usage Highlights

Shang Dynasty:
Bows, arrows, and other daily wares

The Warring States:
Writing tablets

Han Dynasty:
Used to create paper by Cai Lun

Ming Dynasty:
Bamboo charcoal was first documented

Physical and Moral Qualities

Hollow inside
accommodating inner space to embrace new ideas

Phenomenal elasticity
won't break under pressure; sways with adversity

Powerful growth
integrity of purpose; impervious to distraction

Node structure
clear principles not easily compromised

"Better to have a meal without meat than a home without bamboo. Meatless meals make you lose weight, but bambooless homes make you lose sophistication."

— Su Shi

Here is an excerpt from Ji Kang's letter to Shan Tao declining the job offer:

"The Seven Things I Cannot Stand"

1. I like to sleep late, but if I become an official, attendants will wake me early, and this is the first thing I cannot stand.
2. I like to play my *guqin*, shoot birds and catch fish, but if I become an official, attendants will set limits on my movement, and this is the second thing I cannot stand.
3. If I take the position, I have to sit straight at a desk, legs numb with inactivity, unable to scratch the many fleas under my official's robe, and this is the third thing I cannot stand.
4. I'm no good at letter writing, so if I take this position, mail will stack up on my table. And if I don't socialize, it violates customs and manners, and forcing myself to socialize won't last, and this is the fourth thing I cannot stand.
5. I hate funerals, but society takes this tradition seriously, my behavior condemned by people who don't understand me, trying to hurt me for no reason, and yet I cannot change my nature or this situation, and this is the fifth thing I cannot stand.
6. I don't like the masses, but if I take this position, they'll be forced on me, visitors packing my house, a chaotic noisy environment, subjecting me to all kinds of tricks and scams, and this is the sixth thing I cannot stand.
7. I was born impatient, but if I take this position, I will be busy all day, petty political chores always on my mind, and socializing will absorb all my free time, and this is the seventh thing I cannot stand.

Knowing the end was near, Ji Kang implored Shan Tao to watch over his children, a request that Shan Tao honored. Historians recount their relationship as a prime example of "harmony with disagreements between gentlemen" (君子和而不同, *jūnzǐ hé ér bù tóng*). Ji Kang's final act before his execution was to play his *guqin* and sing one last song. His life remains emblematic of an independent-minded scholar who lived life to its fullest, disregarding hollow societal conventions to follow his bliss.

Some Like It Rough

The Sui Dynasty (589–618) endeavored to unify the country once again, following fragmented rule under the Three Kingdoms (220–280), the Western and Eastern Jin (265–402), and the Northern and Southern Dynasties (420–581). The demanding Sui was short-lived, and despite its enormous task of bringing a fractured nation together, segued quickly into the burgeoning Tang Dynasty, just as the ruthless Qin ushered in the prosperous Han. There's that cyclical worldview again.

Many are familiar with the legendary 5th century warrior Mulan, (花木兰, *Huā Mùlán*, 412–502). Disguised as a man, she took the place of her ailing father and went to war against the nomadic Rouran invaders. Twelve years later Mulan returned home a hero, and refused an official post to live the simple life back in her village.

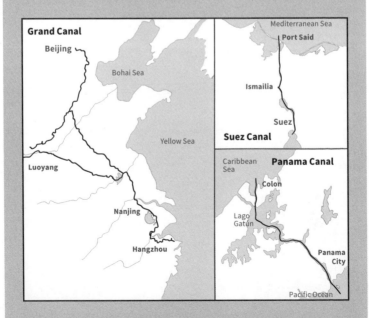

CHINA'S GRAND CANAL: KEY FACTS AND COMPARISONS

The Grand Canal
7th Century

Connected Beijing with Hangzhou, linking the Yellow and Yangtze Rivers and facilitated delivery of key supplies to the Sui Dynasty capital of Luoyang.

Construction began in the year 605 under Emperor Yang of Sui. Five million manual laborers took six years to complete it.

2700km long

30–70m wide

1.2m maximum draft

Opened in 610 and operated for five hundred years. Rerouted and expanded several times; some of its waterways are still operational.

The Suez Canal
19th Century

Connected the Mediterranean and Red Sea shipping lanes through Egypt, eliminating the long journey around South Africa's Cape of Good Hope.

Construction began in 1859 by the French-controlled Suez Canal Company. Labor crews moved 75 million cubic meters of sand to complete it.

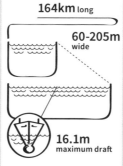

164km long

60–205m wide

16.1m maximum draft

Opened in 1869 and is still operating.

The Panama Canal
19th Century

Connected the Atlantic and Pacific Ocean shipping lanes through Panama, eliminating the hazardous journey around South America's Cape Horn.

Construction began in 1881 under French leadership and was taken over in 1904 by the U.S. 22,000 laborers died of disease and accidents to complete it.

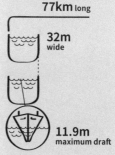

77km long

32m wide

11.9m maximum draft

Opened in 1914 and is still operating.

The Middle Kingdom continued to treat its emperors as living gods with the unquestioned authority to execute anyone for any reason. Sons of Heaven get to call the shots, but they also catch all the blame for earthquakes, floods, droughts, plagues, and other random acts of nature.

What's more, when the peasants faced mass starvation or were forced to endure extreme amounts of incompetence and corruption, almost any natural disaster could be construed as a "vote of no confidence" from the heavens and convenient rationale for violent overthrow.

The most notorious of the Sui rulers was Yangdi (隋炀帝, *Suí Yángdì*, 569–618), remembered both for his brutality (he is said to have murdered his emperor father and his brothers) and his extravagance (he apparently spent far too much time riding around on barges full of concubines). Yangdi mobilized 5.4 million laborers to complete the Grand Canal, and also reconstructed the Great Wall. He fought disastrous battles with China's neighbors and lost several times to the Goguryeo nation, based in what is now Pyongyang, North Korea. The deaths of millions of his people to hardship, disease, and warfare, coupled with his crippling taxation policies, led to the precipitous downfall of the dynasty and places Yangdi on the shortlist for China's worst emperor award.

Love-Hate Relationship

One fascinating aspect of the Sui-Tang era, often linked by historians as one extended dynasty, was the prevalence of intermarriages between the ruling Yang and Li families. Here's one sequence of Macbeth-like relationships that might have caused even Shakespeare to knock over his ink bottle: The Sui first emperor's wife's sister gave birth to a son who would become the Tang first emperor, that is, the Sui first emperor's nephew. This first Tang emperor married his cousin, a niece of the Sui emperor, and gave birth to a second Tang emperor, who also married a Sui cousin. The second Tang emperor consolidated power by killing two brothers and all ten of their sons, then demanded his father, the first Tang emperor, step aside in a not-unfamiliar moment, given this father had previously toppled his mom's sister's husband, his beloved uncle.

Paraphrasing Sir William: There is nothing either good or bad, but ain't karma a bitch? This elitist coupling might have produced some wickedly dangerous DNA had not the ruling families themselves been products of ethnic Han intermarriage with Turkic and Mongolic nomadic tribal families. The resulting multiethnic leaders retained Han surnames and ruled during the Tang under the banner of Chinese tradition.

Poets, Prophets, and Pulchritude

Living large in the Tang Dynasty

*"Christian, Jew, Muslim, shaman, Zoroastrian,
stone, ground, mountain, river; each has
a secret way of being with the mystery,
unique and not to be judged."*

— Rumi

"If you meet the Buddha on the road, kill him."

— Linji Yixuan

SUI-TANG ERA TIMELINE

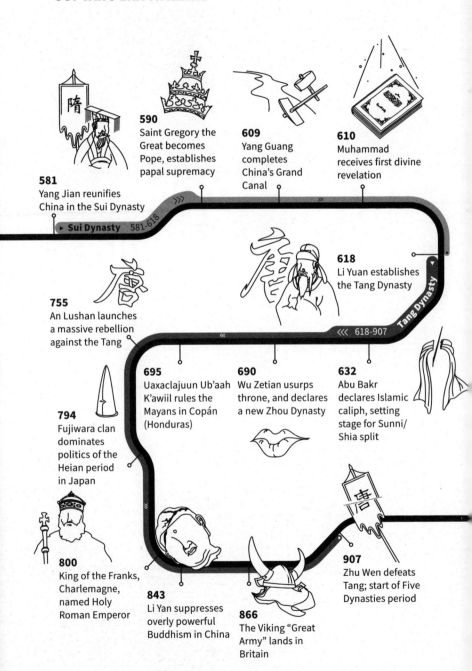

Welcome to the romantic, the splendid, the magnificent Tang! Chinese adore this dynasty and consider it a golden age in Chinese civilization. Some believe today's China is heading towards a Tang-like resurgence of innovation, trade, and ideas. Let's see for ourselves if the Tang can live up to the hype.

The Tang Dynasty (618–907) was an era of wine, women, and song, plus poetry, literature, art, science, and medicine, featuring more pathways to the divine than ever before. As Europe wallowed in its Dark Ages (500–1100), China globalized and continued the astounding streak of innovation that started in the Han Dynasty. Powerful trade, political stability, and official appointments based on an imperial examination system boosted the Middle Kingdom's economy to an estimated 60% of global GDP. Whoa: That's more than today's United States, European Union, Japan, and India combined.

With over 1.5 million people, Chang'an (present day Xi'an) was the planet's most populous city, a bustling, multi-cultural metropolis. The earlier trickle of Silk Road traders was now a flood of ambitious immigrants seeking fortunes in a brave new world. Tang records note that an Arab once earned the highest degree on the civil service examination. And foreigners held plenty of positions within the Tang legislative bureau, a reflection of the dynasty's cultural openness and the multiethnic bloodlines of the ruling Li family. When China feels confident, it opens to the world.

The All-Stars of Enlightenment

The most influential foreigner in China's history came to prominence during the Tang. He traveled in spirit along the Silk Road from the Han Dynasty onwards and his revolutionary beliefs were transported to China through oral storytelling traditions of the time. It's ironic that the Chinese, who never met this Indian prince, were so captivated by his coherent guidance on how to escape earthly suffering. We're talking, of course, about Siddhārtha Gautama, the Buddha.

Buddhism and Daoism were instant brothers—release of desire, selfless inner peace, no creator gods—and provided spiritual comfort in a chaotic world. Chinese monks translated Pali scriptures using recognized Daoist terms to cross-pollinate with familiar doctrine, then passed these new texts to Korea, Japan, and Vietnam. Buddhism also introduced the concept of reincarnation, which matched the dominant cyclical view and infused Daoism with renewed energy.

The wildest theories hold that Laozi journeyed to India to meet Buddha and talk philosophy, or that perhaps Buddha was a reincarnation of Laozi himself! While most historians dismiss those notions as idle speculation, there remain some striking parallels in thinking between these two sages:

| Laozi wrote:
道可道，非常道。
名可名，非常名。
The Way that can be expressed is not the everlasting Way;
Names that can be named are not changeless Names. | Buddha wrote:
言语道断。
The Way is beyond language;
The Highest Principle cannot be explained in words. |

Daoism and Buddhism received the most attention during the Tang, though other religions thrived as well, driven by social tolerance and receptivity to new ideas. The Nestorians, a sect of Christianity banned by the Romans, followed the Silk Road to settle in China, where they practiced through to the 14th century. Islam found a home in the heart of China as well, introduced by the maternal uncle of Mohammed in the decades following the death of the Prophet. Later, a Tang emperor built China's first mosque in Guangzhou.

> *"To conquer oneself is a greater task than conquering others."*
>
> — Buddha

BUDDHISM IN TWO EQUATIONS:

Change × Resistance = Suffering
Nirvana = Meditation + Awareness + Release

Buddha's Four Noble Truths demystified:
1. Life is dissatisfying because all things are impermanent and cannot provide lasting happiness.
2. We suffer because we attach to self-centered desires.
3. Suffering ceases when we detach from desire and live with compassion for all living things.
4. The path to end suffering is based on wisdom, ethical conduct, and meditation.

In other words, enjoy the roller coaster ride of life, but don't reach out and grab anything!

Let's attempt to put things in perspective using a basketball analogy: If Buddha became the all-star center in the Tang spiritual starting five, could we say that Jesus and Mohammed were the starting guards in his back court? To the Chinese, Buddhism proved more adaptable and controllable. The ubiquitous Buddha stone carvings in Luoyang and Leshan testify that, during this era, Buddhism outshone Confucianism by embracing all levels of society. While Jesus and Mohammed were highly respected sages within the Tang pantheon, Christianity and Islam were unable to capture the mass imagination of the time, possibly because their jealous monotheistic gods lacked popular appeal when compared to the localized assortment of go-to deities. But in retrospect, our basketball all-star analogy was poorly chosen—feed the ball inside to Buddha and he might contemplate its roundness rather than dunk it.

And what about Chinese Buddhist monk Linji's chapter-opening quote advising us, should we meet the Buddha on the road, to kill him? That's only spiritual-speak for: "When you think you've finally found true enlightenment, release that thought and keep meditating."

Sisters Are Doin' It for Themselves

The Tang was also a golden age for smart, driven women. Two in particular stand out, for vastly different reasons: the domineering Wu Zetian, China's first and only female emperor, and the curvaceous Yang Guifei, one of China's legendary Four Great Beauties.

Wu Zetian (武则天, *Wǔ Zétiān*, 624–705) became China's first and only female emperor through a series of clever Machiavellian moves. Once in power, she pushed through reforms and expanded the empire's footprint, zapping the Goguryeo, the Korean nation that had defeated the Sui. She earned respect for her solid judgment, and gave birth to three sons who also became emperors.

But how did she get there? Wu was a precocious child: She hated needlepoint but enjoyed reading and travel with her parents. Her beauty (and her family's standing in society) quickly brought her to the attention of Emperor Taizong, who sent envoys to recruit her as a royal consort when she was thirteen. Her mother wept as she was taken away to live in the imperial palace, but Wu, already displaying the practical thinking that would bring her to power, consoled her by saying, "How do you know it's not my fortune to meet the Son of Heaven?" Wu's mother might cry, but she must have also been secretly thrilled: Having your daughter chosen as a imperial concubine was like your family winning the lottery, with conditions: She might one day become a prized empress, or she might make the wrong move and get your entire family executed.

WU ZETIAN ASCENDS TO POWER

Concubine Wu: Chosen at age 13

Consort Wu: Companion to the late emperor's son

Empress Wu: Eliminated reigning Empress and became strong influence on husband

Empress Dowager Wu: Ruled behind the curtain of her husband and 2 sons

Emperor Wu: Crowned as China's first and only female emperor at age 67

Wu Zetian became a trusted confidant to both Emperor Taizong and his ninth son, the next Emperor Gaozong. Some historians surmise that she was already sleeping with the son when Dad was alive. Bucking the traditional role of consort, she advised both men on their military campaigns and matters of social importance. Consort Wu became so valued as a legitimate source of good political advice that, although she never bore sons to either man, she was able to remain in court. (Concubines who didn't bear sons were sent to the convent to become nuns upon the Emperor's death.) Somehow, she also managed to dodge Confucian prohibitions against sharing a bed with a dead man's son.

> "I need only three things
> to subdue a defiant horse:
> an iron whip, an iron hammer,
> and a sharp dagger.
> I'll whip it with the iron whip.
> If it doesn't submit,
> I'll hammer its head with the iron hammer.
> If it still doesn't submit,
> I'll cut its throat with the dagger."
>
> — Wu Zetian

Consort Wu had a real flair for not letting the truth derail her ambitions. She made multiple attempts to unseat Gaozong's wife, Empress Wang, accusing her of practicing witchcraft and plotting treason. It's said Consort Wu even strangled her own newborn daughter and pinned it on the Empress! Once Emperor Gaozong caved in and demoted Empress Wang, the new Empress Wu had the former empress executed, along with all others who had opposed her ascent. Empress Wu later claimed their angry ghosts tormented her for years.

FAMOUS FEMALE LEADERS

	Cleopatra VII	**Wu Zetian**	**Elizabeth I**
lived from	69–30 BC	624–705	1533–1603
saw herself as	reincarnation of the Egyptian goddess Isis	Maitreya, a future incarnation of Buddha	the "illegitimate" daughter of King Henry VIII and Ann Bolyn
most famous for	ruling as Pharaoh in Ptolemy Egypt	starting her own dynasty	returning England to Protestantism
married	her two brothers named Ptolemy	father and son emperors	no one (refused political marriages)
hot relationships	Caesar Augustus, Marc Anthony	the Buddhist monk Huaiyi	remained "the virgin queen"
thorn in her side	Roman civil wars	feckless male heirs to throne	Bloody Mary's Protestant purges

Being number two in command wasn't enough. Impatient with Gaozong's ineffectual leadership, she forced her influence onto every major decision. Gaozong's premature demise (oops! Where did that poison come from?) and a series of feckless replacements paved the way for Wu Zetian to declare herself first emperor of a new dynasty, complete with an Orwellian legion of secret police and informants. Somewhere along the way she also began an affair with a monk, which likely influenced her to advance Buddhism over Taoism and Confucianism in policy during her reign. Some historians portray Wu Zetian as a paranoid control freak, but it's worth considering: How different was she from earlier male paranoid control freaks?

The Beginning of the End

Emperor Xuanzong (唐玄宗, *Táng Xuánzōng*, 685–762), a grandson of Wu Zetian, ruled for 42 years at the Tang's pinnacle of prosperity. Xuanzong presided over glorious state ceremonies and promoted further cultural development. He was also an accomplished musician who composed dance music for the court ladies and, it's even been said, trained his horses to dance holding wine cups in their mouths. Xuanzong struggled with overspending on the military and underreporting of taxes, along with a loss of control to his military governors and mercenary armies along the empire's periphery. It was a problem that would later come back to haunt him.

With the tens of thousands of women kept for him in the imperial palace, Xuanzong fathered a total of 30 sons and 29 daughters. Still, the one woman who truly captured his heart was Yang Guifei (杨贵妃, *Yáng Guìfēi*, 719–756), one of China's Four Great Beauties. Problem was, this Rubenesque teenager was already married to Xuanzong's son, Prince Li. Naturally, Prince Li wasn't crazy about his old man stealing his young bride, but hey, Dad did the decent thing and found him a new one. To avoid accusations of impropriety, Xuanzong ordered Yang Guifei to become a nun, thus disconnecting her from their family, and then snuck her back into the imperial palace as his new favorite consort.

Once together, the happy couple went through one rocky separation after another with great predictability: she says something to enrage him; he banishes her from the palace; she goes into a deep funk; he can't eat or sleep. Xuanzong finally summons her back. And repeat. The royal psychiatrists must have been on call 24-7.

> *"When the show ends, the puppet is cast aside;*
> *it's as short as the dream of a lifetime."*
>
> — Xuanzong Emperor

Xuanzong may have survived heartache to win his great love, but his biggest headache was about to start. The calamity was caused by his and Yang Guifei's favorite adopted son, their Turkish general, An Lushan, who controlled 160,000 troops in the north. Perhaps prompted by fears about his own fate after the elder Xuanzong's death, An Lushan seized control of the capital, Chang'an, and declared himself the new emperor. Blindsided, Xuanzong and his retinue fled for Chengdu. On the road, Xuanzong's loyal soldiers confronted him with the stark reality: Yang Guifei and her now-powerful family had caused An Lushan to rebel. Filled with grief and unable to resist, Xuanzong had Yang Guifei taken to a Buddhist shrine and strangled.

The An Lushan rebellion was an eight-year disaster from which the Tang Dynasty never recovered. Pre-rebellion, in 754, the census recorded 53 million people; ten years later it recorded only 17 million. Thirty-six million Chinese citizens had been killed or permanently displaced in the chaos. It is China's second-highest official wartime death toll behind the Second Sino-Japanese War, nearly 1200 years later.

When faced with a profound loss of power and influence, China often turns inward to its core values, such as Confucianism, and blames foreign ideas and outside influences for its misfortunes. During the Tang Dynasty's decline, that foreign influence was Buddhism. Monasteries once seen as integral parts of society were implicated for their extensive tax-exempt land holdings

CHINA'S FOUR GREAT BEAUTIES

Legend has it that their powerful beauty could sink fish in lakes, fell geese from the sky, eclipse the moon, and put flowers to shame. Can you imagine the havoc their downloads would wreak upon today's sensitive mobile devices?

Xi Shi

was famous for her wily charms during the Spring and Autumn period. Living abroad with the enemy king, she so distracted him that his army was crushed and he took his own life. Xi Shi returned to frolic in the mists of Lake Tai, at least in the fairy tale.

Wang Zhaojun

was an accidental hero of the Han era. Because the royal portrait artist painted her ugly, the emperor gave her away by mistake to a visiting Xiongnu prince. The valiant Zhaojun facilitated 60 years of peace between China and the Xiongnu along the northern front.

Diaochan

was a character (based on a real person) in Romance of the Three Kingdoms caught in a juicy love triangle. The jealous warrior kills the warlord, then is killed by warlord's posse. The ravishing Diaochan ends up with a possessive general whose friends adore her, so the general kills her.

Yang Guifei

was a Tang Dynasty dazzler who first married a handsome prince, then married his possessive father, the emperor. In the end, her political naiveté cost her dearly. There's even a song many school kids can sing about the doomed love between an emperor and his consort.

and business dealings. In the ensuing repression, nearly 50,000 Buddhist structures were seized, and a quarter million monks and nuns forcibly reassigned to lay life. But as aristocratic family domination waned, Tang society creative expression blossomed among the political dysfunction and decay.

Social Media in the Tang

Imagine an art form at its peak of potency. A means of expression to capture complex emotions, everything from heartfelt aspirations to desperate longings to random musings. That was the role filled by Tang poetry.

When you left home on a journey—a frightening proposition in the aftermath of the An Lushan rebellion—there was a near-total communication disconnect. You had no idea if you would ever see your loved ones again. Poetry was the ideal outlet for your deepest hopes and fears.

The Tang poets took China's ancient freestyle poetry form, then experimented and innovated around it to create entirely new boundaries of rhyme and meter. Some say that the canon of Tang poetry started out by describing mountains, progressed to conversing on politics, and ended up talking about love. Along the way, poets emerged from all backgrounds, from aristocrats to monks. Even government officials in the late Tang to early Song dynasties were required to pass a test consisting of classical poetry composition, calligraphic writing, and mastery of a musical instrument. How things have changed!

In the late Tang, the real fun took place in the clubs. An aspiring poet might spend weeks sweating over a verse in anticipation of a public reading, while another would just scribble out a few riffs, then entreat a lovely courtesan to sing them with musical accompaniment. In terms of societal impact, late Tang into Song-era poetic performance was akin to a modern collision of rap and jazz. And it was huge.

The Tang poets were a prolific lot. The *Complete Collection of Tang Poetry* contains a whopping 42,863 poems by 2,529 poets spread over 900 volumes. Reading the entire collection, at a pace of three new poems per day, would take you almost 40 years. Fortunately, for schoolkids of the 21st century, the more portable *300 Tang Poems* is often one of the first books gifted to them by their parents.

Two of the most respected Tang poets, Du Fu and Li Bai, drew upon a similar palette of events and experiences, yet each infused his verse with different meaning. Du Fu (杜甫, *Dù Fǔ*, 712–770) explored the societal themes of separation and loyalty; the impermanence of the human condition, and nature's indifference to human suffering to provide a collective sense of Chinese identity during the Tang decline. Known as the "Poet Sage," Du Fu's 1,500 preserved poems, many with Confucian leanings, continue to grow in popularity.

The literary brilliance of Li Bai (李白, *Lǐ Bái*, 701–762) attracted the attention of Emperor Xuanzong, who hired him as a translator. It soon became clear this nonconformist was too much like the

TAO YUANMING: THE POET'S POET

Tao Yuanming (陶淵明, Táo Yuānmíng) lived in chaotic times during the Eastern Jin Dynasty (317–420). A master of the Pastoral style, Tao explored the virtues of solitude. He longed for harmony with nature and connection with the senses.

The preface to his famous poem *Peach Blossom Spring* describes a fisherman who discovers a secluded village utopia. He promises the villagers to keep its location a secret. But when he tries to return, the fisherman is unable to find the place ever again.

Considered the archetypal Chinese intellectual, Tao also inspired the American Beat Poets of the 1960s. Known for his uncompromising lifestyle, Tao once said, "I will not bow like a servant for five bushels of grain."

THE TANG GIANTS: DU FU AND LI BAI

Moon Night Missing My Brother
War drums interrupt life on the streets,
far in the frontier autumn cry the wild geese;
from tonight on the dew will turn white,
only in homeland is the moon bright;
brothers are spread near and far,
without news on their whereabouts;
letters often go missing on the way,
the ongoing war only makes it worse.

《月夜忆舍弟》
戍鼓断人行，边秋一雁声
露从今夜白，月是故乡明
有弟皆分散，无家问死生
寄书长不达，况乃未休兵

杜甫
Du Fu
The realist

A skilled calligrapher whose unexpected failure on the civil service exam led him to a life of poetry (lucky for us).

李白
Li Bai
The romantic

His imaginative and playful style, reviving past poetic traditions, was fueled by his free-spirited drinking.

《将进酒》
君不见黄河之水天上来，
奔流到海不复回。
君不见高堂明镜悲白发，
朝如青丝暮成雪。
人生得意须尽欢，
莫使金樽空对月。

Bring On The Wine!
See you not the waters of
the Yellow River rushing from on high,
racing to the sea never to return?
See you not the sad aged locks
in bright mirrors of high halls,
dark at dawn to white by night?
Make as merry as you wish while you can,
never let a golden goblet lie empty
in the moonlight.

philsopher Zhuangzi, who also disputed the value of worldly pursuits and was a poor fit with the Imperial Palace. After he was booted out of the capital, Li Bai deepened his connection with Daoism and became known as the "Wandering Poet" and one of the "Eight Immortals of the Wine Cup." Legend has it that Li Bai drowned in the Yangtze River, bombed out of his mind, while trying to catch the moon's reflection.

The Melancholy Murderer

Let's explore one more Tang poet. You won't find her in *300 Tang Poems*. Nor was she eulogized for transcendent verse or keen social observations. To the contrary, Yu Xuanji (鱼玄机, *Yú Xuánjī*, 844–868) lived the flamboyant life of a courtesan.

If her story were a Hollywood film, we would open with Ms. Yu kneeling on the ground, surrounded by condescending faces, asked by some magistrate if she has any last words before her execution. We would then flashback to the story of a woman living in a period of relative female freedom and opportunity. We would see that her authenticity and candor touched the lives of many, especially those she inspired to break free from their perceived and societal limitations.

The movie would also have to address the villains of the plot, Yu Xuanji's critics, who point to the profound inner conflict between her staunch Daoist practice and her powerful emotions, which found outlet only through her poetry. And what about the murder of which Yu was accused? When her maid declared, "I haven't been with any men since arriving at this Daoist compound," Yu took it as mocking her own professed virtue. She flipped out and murdered her maid. History records this as the source of her madness.

Yu Xuanji's "my life is an open book" style of autobiographical poetry addressed subjects from unrequited love to the rising price of peonies, even the wistfulness of watching her own hair turn gray. Her 40–50 published poems earned her a section in the *Complete Collection of Tang Poetry*.

YU XUANJI   1st
Tang poet and performance artist
Chang'an, China | Entertainment

Dynamic rennaissance woman with diverse experiences:
• Concubine to a high-flying official, conversant on all current events.
• Daoist nun with deep appreciation for feminist issues and contemporary female roles in a changing society.
• Courtesan skilled in poetic composition (including popular 5-character variation), plus engaging onstage delivery of third-party verse.
References available on request. Follow me on Weibo and Twitter!

Send a message

500+ connections

https://cn.linkedin.com/yuxuanji/zh-cn   Contact Info

Here is Yu Xuanji's emotional response to a married friend's poem, who presumably was trying to build some distance from her:

A "Summer Fishing" Matching Poem to Li Ying
by Yu Xuanji

Living on the same street and never again seeing each other. Pure poems to an old flame, new branches for a scented cassia.
The eternal Dao has no time for my ephemeral ice and snow nature, the Zen simplicity mocks my silk and gauze extravagance. My footprints ascend to the heavens, but no path connects my spiritual waves and mist.

《酬李郢夏日钓鱼回见示》
鱼玄机

住处虽同巷，
经年不一过。
清词劝旧女，
香桂折新柯。
道性欺冰雪，
禅心笑绮罗。
迹登霄汉上，
无路接烟波。

Even the most talented writers of today struggle to recapture the magic of a Tang verse, since those poetic boundaries were based on the unique dialect of the time. There's an old saying that goes: If you can recite 300 Tang poems, even if you can't pen one of your own, at least you'll be able to sing along. So as we approach the end of our journey through the Tang Dynasty, let us raise our glasses high and drink a toast to the myriad of poets and artists who make our world a more beautiful place.

A Farewell to a Friend
by Li Bai

Blue mountains stretch beyond the north wall, clear water curves east of the city.
Here is where you depart, a rootless dandelion on a ten thousand mile journey.
Thoughts of a drifter are like floating clouds, into the sunset an old friendship drifts away.
As we wave our hands to say farewell again and again our horses neigh.

《送友人》
李白

青山横北郭,
白水绕东城。
此地一为别,
孤蓬万里征。
浮云游子意,
落日故人情。
挥手自兹去,
萧萧班马鸣。

SEVEN

Why Rule When You Can Be an Artiste?

The Song Dynasty cultural explosion

"Whenever reading history, it is necessary not merely to remember the facts, but also to become aware of the principles of good government and disorder, security and danger, rise and fall, survival and destruction."

— Cheng Yi

"Art is the lie that tells the truth."

— Pablo Picasso

SONG ERA TIMELINE

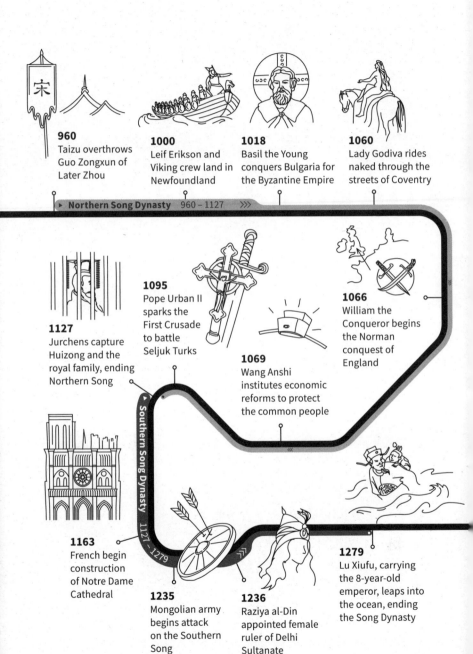

Along the River During the Qingming Festival, a work painted by court artist Zhang Zeduan during the Northern Song Dynasty (960–1127), has been called China's *Mona Lisa* for the wide acclaim heaped upon it over the ages. Because of its fragility, the priceless scroll is seldom displayed, even in Beijing, and has never been loaned for an overseas exhibition. This 17.32-foot (5.28-meter) painting conveys the full spectrum of life in and around the capital city of Kaifeng. The realistic piece contrasts sharply with the older *shanshui* (山水, lit. "mountain water") landscape style, which revered misty mountains and reflected how miniscule most Daoists felt in the bigger picture of nature and of life.

Let's Hear It for the Average Zhou!

The major significance of Zhang's brushed-ink masterpiece stems from its portrayal of common people, who were beginning to have relevance and means for advancement in society. The scenes captured in *Along the River* contain exactly 814 people and many animals—but no pandas. Pandas didn't appear in Chinese art until the 20th century. And how, you might ask, do we know the exact number of people in Zhang's painting? Because someone enamored with Zhang Zeduan's masterwork once spent an entire afternoon placing individual grains of rice, with painstaking precision, on every single body in the scroll. He then swept up the rice and counted the grains.

Song Huizong, the "Artist Emperor" (more on him in a moment), fell in love with *Along the River* the moment he saw it. The last emperor, Puyi, absconded with the scroll when he fled the Forbidden City near the end of the Qing Dynasty. All told, *Along the River* was stolen five times from the imperial palace.

Along the River struck a humanistic chord to match the cultural vibe of the Northern Song and heralded an emerging school of art that specialized in depictions of the ordinary. Following five decades of post-Tang fragmented rule, the Tang's military and aristocratic elite yielded to Song's bureaucratic scholar elite. This era also witnessed the resurgence of Confucian ideals and the

ART IMITATES LIFE

Zhang Zeduan's masterpiece *Along the River During the Qingming Festival* captured the zeitgeist of the Northern Song Dynasty, when the life of the common Chinese was imbued with existential and artistic significance.

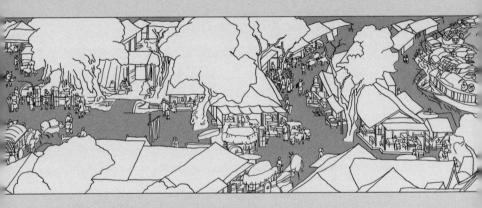

The capital of Kaifeng was home to over 1,000,000 people (fewer than 500,000 lived in Constantinople). China's overall population was 100 million, with over 20% living as urban residents (the UK didn't reach that level until 1795), an all-time record for China's dynastic era.

One night, the fourth Song Emperor, Renzong, heard music and laughter outside the palace. "Where is that noise coming from?" asked the emperor. "That's the sound of entertainment in the local pub," said the maid. The emperor reflected, "People outside enjoy themselves, while inside we have a stable work life with little entertainment." The maid said, "It's because you work hard that people outside can relax and enjoy themselves."

imperial exam, which has echoes in China's modern *gaokao* (高考) college entrance exam.

In response to dangers along the northern frontiers and an ongoing southern business expansion, the North-to-South migration accelerated. Increasingly, people turned to rice farming in the fertile South, which expanded the food supply. China's population surpassed the 100-million mark, leading historian Patricia Buckley Ebrey to conclude that China's share of world population in the year 1100 was likely even higher than in modern times. Some have compared this sustained movement with the westward migration in American history and the eastward migration in Russian history.

The emergence of a gentry class, the advancement of individual free enterprise, a nascent service industry, and a lighter governmental touch on the markets all helped business to thrive. Finally, the invention of moveable type caused a massive cultural leap forward. For the first time in world history, printed money fueled transactions, and vast numbers of printed books powered minds.

While the business and artistic fascination unfolded, an increasingly powerful three-pronged barbarian threat loomed to the north. The Song emperors overspent on defense, including new gunpowder weapons, but failed to maintain a military advantage as their innovations were quickly copied by Tangut and Khitan adversaries. Left with no easy way out, the Song rulers paid off their nomadic northern neighbors with land, metals, and silk. What's more, the pacifist Confucian administration didn't exactly respect their military leadership. The administrators gave the generals just enough power to hold the barbarians at bay, but not enough to entertain notions of overthrowing their own government. Nobody within the Song political sphere wanted to face the frustrating reality that China had little hope of regaining its dominance and swagger from the Han and Tang eras.

INNER ASIA TRIBES

Chinese history books often refer to them as "barbarians," but these powerful tribes established Chinese dynasties and left significant imprints on Chinese culture:

Xiongnu 匈奴

A confederation of mixed nomadic peoples who controlled huge territories on Han China's northern frontier and extracted tribute from its emperors. Attila the Hun may have been a descendant.

Tibetans 吐蕃

At its peak, the Tibetan empire (618–842) held most of what is now Western China, battling Tang emperors, even occupying the capital of Chang'an. Their empire later collapsed following a civil war.

Khitans 契丹

Mongol-like nomadic peoples who founded the Liao Dynasty (907–1125) in the north, which had a larger landmass than Song China. They were later defeated by the Jurchens.

Tanguts 党项

Multiethnic peoples who migrated into Northwest China to establish the Western Xia Dynasty (1038–1227). The Mongols destroyed their civilization, but the Tanguts likely killed Genghis Khan.

Jurchens 女真

Manchu peoples who conquered North China to form the Jin Dynasty (1125–1234), later defeated by the Mongols. In the 17th century, the Manchus aligned with the Mongols to defeat the Ming and rule China under the Qing Dynasty banner.

Mongols 蒙古

Nomadic peoples of mixed ancestry united by Genghis Khan, which later conquered all of China to found the Yuan Dynasty (1271–1368) and occupy the largest contiguous land empire in history.

Never Mind Those Urgent Messages …
Pass Me That Paint Brush

The Song Dynasty's self-perpetuating bureaucracy, coupled with a regional stalemate, ushered in one of the most self-indulgent eras in Chinese history. And the poster child for *la dolce vita* was Huizong (宋徽宗, *Sòng Huīzōng,* 1082–1135), the eighth Song ruler, often called the "artist emperor."

Huizong favored vibrant cultural expression over all those annoying responsibilities. An accomplished painter, poet, musician, calligrapher, designer, and tea connoisseur, Huizong established an Imperial Painting Academy and presided over one of the golden ages of Chinese painting. His royal art collection comprised over 6,000 paintings. Huizong's own paintings have been curated into New York's Metropolitan Museum of Art and many other fine-art institutions. He produced over 15,000 pieces himself, the career equivalent of perhaps twenty artists, leading some historians to surmise that court artists assisted with some of the painting. Huizong drove his fellow artists nuts with his obsession to aesthetic detail: "No! Peacocks move *this* way, not that way."

> *"There's nothing he (Song Huizong) cannot do … except rule as emperor."*
>
> — History of Song

Apple's founder Steve Jobs would have loved this guy. All the way back in the Song Dynasty, Huizong created his own font! He even made it legal for talented artists to wear purple robes, the same color robes as high-ranking officials. (Note to self: still forbidden to wear gold robes; gets you killed.) As a dynastic leader, however, Huizong left a lot to be desired: Buddhist philosophers speculate that Huizong somehow incarnated into the wrong body, and ended up on the throne by mistake. Imagine living under Mozart as Archbishop of Salzburg, or Oscar Wilde as a Marquess on the

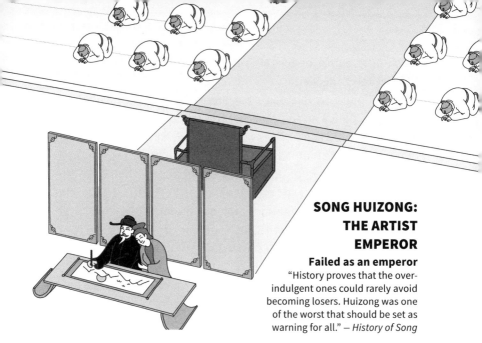

SONG HUIZONG: THE ARTIST EMPEROR

Failed as an emperor

"History proves that the over-indulgent ones could rarely avoid becoming losers. Huizong was one of the worst that should be set as warning for all." — *History of Song*

The Northern Song Dynasty ended after 25 years under his reign.

Succeeded as an artist

❶ Project leader full of creative ideas for painting and art projects

❷ An accomplished painter

❸ A highly talented poet

❹ A creative calligrapher

❺ Founder of the Royal Academy of Fine Arts

❻ Art educator who created an education and selection system for art training

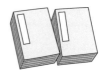

❼ Chief editor of the imperial painting catalogue, featuring more than 6,000 paintings

❽ Huizong was passionate about music, culture, landscape design, and seemingly anything that has nothing to do with the responsibility of running an empire.

Irish Privy Council, or Elvis as President of the United States. Huge fun; wicked hangover.

Many point to Huizong's preference for art and negligence of foreign policy as the cause of the fall of the Northern Song in 1127. But it wasn't all his fault. After all, Huizong, like all the emperors before him, relied on the guidance of his top advisors. When a large wave of Jurchen invaders approached from the north, Huizong panicked and fled the capital. He returned after the Jurchens' failed first siege attempt, but during the second siege, he was captured along with 3,000 members of his family and royal entourage. Huizong's ninth son escaped to Hangzhou to become the first emperor of the Southern Song Dynasty.

Huizong toiled along at the hands of his captors for the final eight years of his life. But don't feel too badly for him. All in, he sired 32 sons and 34 daughters, and even managed to father an additional 19 kids while in captivity. (Don't ask, they might not all be his.) Among the 557 Chinese emperors, Huizong's total of 85 descendants remains an unmatched record of procreative prowess.

Bound for Obscurity

The growth of Confucianism and return to traditional roles in the Southern Song Dynasty (1127–1279) was the reaction to this sudden loss of power, just as religious fundamentalism tends to thrive where people feel most threatened by rapid change and an uncertain future. These "neo-Confucian" scholars were influenced by Buddhist concepts: They rejected superstition and sought rationality through core Chinese elements, thus reconnecting in spirit to the glory days of the Han Dynasty and basking in the warmth of cultural superiority.

In their overzealous quest for a disciplined social order, the authorities came up with a preponderance of life prescriptions. *Precepts for Social Life*, authored by one Song official, details two hundred cultural topics requiring added guidance, including how to get along with your relatives, how to discipline your son, and how to beat a servant (hint: don't do it yourself).

The official offers this sage advice: "The general rule with maids and concubines is to be careful of what is begun and take precautions concerning how things might end."

Remember the active female archetype of the Tang Dynasty? How very last millennium of you. Southern Song Dynasty society began to close the door on women's social freedom. By the Ming Dynasty, two centuries later, women would have almost no outside life.

Nonetheless, women's voices were still heard. Li Qingzhao (李清照, *Lǐ Qīngzhào*, 1084–1151), a Song Dynasty writer born into a literary family, penned love poems in her native Shandong province. After the Jurchens destroyed their home, Qingzhao and her husband fled south, where she gave voice to the frustrations of her generation, such as weak Song emperors unable to defend their beloved land. Chinese history now regards Qingzhao as its greatest female poet. There are even impact craters on Mercury and Venus named after her.

Lines Written On A Summer's Day
by Li Qingzhao

《夏日绝句》
李清照

*In life we should be heroes
among the living;
after death, let us be heroes
among the ghosts.
To this day we miss that
ancient hero Xiang Yu,
who would rather die than
cross the East River in
retreat.*

生当作人杰，
死亦为鬼神。
至今思项羽，
不肯过江东。

The Southern Song's definition of beauty is exemplified by a delicate, stay-at-home woman with tiny bound feet, her dainty veiled movements heightening her attractiveness as a potential bride. Foot-binding itself started in the royal court, spread to the upper class, and later, even to peasant women, who must have found it exceedingly difficult to slosh around in the paddy fields. What is so attractive about bound feet, anyway? Song social records indicate divided male opinion on their erotic appeal: The more fetishistic enjoyed the bare clenched foot's peculiar look and doughy feel, while the more conservative kept his wife's tootsies under wraps, better left to the imagination.

Modern observers question how such a practice could have continued unabated into 19th-century China. Comparisons have been made with waist-cinching among Victorian women and forced labia minora elongation among African girls. In England, as late as 1865, a prominent gynecologist called for removal of the clitoris, saying that its "unnatural irritation" caused epilepsy, hysteria and/or mania. Clearly, the Chinese were not alone in questionable practices forced onto their female population.

A Hero For The Ages

General Yue Fei (岳飞, *Yuè Fēi,* 1103–1142) rekindled China's dream of recapturing its lost territories in the north. Yue Fei's origins are nothing short of cinematic: His father sacrificed himself during a flood on the Yellow River by ensuring the Yue Fei and his mother were safely afloat in a large clay jar before looking after his own safety. As a youth, Yue Fei excelled in martial arts under the master Zhou Tong. Later, he invented his own style of spear fighting and became proficient in the Eagle Claw kung fu form portrayed in Quentin Tarantino's film *Kill Bill*. (Yes, it's for real). Before entering the military, his mother tattooed characters that read "loyally serve the country" onto his back.

Yue Fei formed an independent unit of like-minded soldiers, raided Jurchen strongholds and earned a reputation as an unshakable military leader. After ten years of successful campaigns, during which he reclaimed a portion of China's heartland from the Jurchens, Yue Fei was summoned to the capital by the Emperor. Yue Fei expected praise for his work, but instead was executed. Accounts differ as to exactly how, but the why isn't in question—the Emperor feared that if Yue Fei captured the former Northern Song capital of Kaifeng from the Jurchens, it might prompt the release of the real heir to the Song throne, the Emperor's older brother. Yue Fei was sacrificed out of self-interest, plus a deal for peace with the Jurchens, which bought another 137 years for the Southern Song. Yue Fei did not die in vain; he was later given the honorific title of a Hubei king and immortalized as a symbol of resistance, loyalty, and honor.

> "My wrath bristles through my helmet,
> the rain stops as I stand by the rain;
> I look up towards the sky and let loose a passionate roar.
> Let us ride our chariots through the Helan Pass ...
> there we shall feast on barbarian flesh
> and drink (enemy) blood.
> Let us begin anew to recover our
> old empire before paying tribute to the Emperor."
>
> — Yue Fei

The curtain closed on the Southern Song Dynasty in 1279 at Yamen, near the Pearl River Delta in Guangdong Province. This is the site of the Mongol navy's defeat of the Song. The Mongols, leaders of the incoming Yuan Dynasty, were outnumbered ten-to-one, yet prevailed through superior tactics.

When defeat was imminent, a desperate Song chancellor named Lu Xiufu strapped the dynasty's final emperor, 8-year-old Zhao Bing, onto his back and leapt from their boat into the ocean, drowning them both. Family and Song loyalists followed, until tens of thousands of bodies were left floating in the South China Sea.

The Greatest Military Leader in History

Genghis Khan (1162–1227) founded the Mongol Empire, a collection of nomadic tribes united in the shared goal of conquest. So far-reaching were his exploits that experts believe his Y-chromosome is now present in one of every two hundred people on the planet. Just as incredible is the fact that Genghis Khan conquered more lands and people in 25 years than the Romans did in 400 years. That's more than twice as much as any man in history. But he never conquered China. Genghis Khan's grandson, Kublai, accomplished that feat 50 years later using a combination of Mongol ingenuity and political adaptation to make his Yuan (meaning "origin") Dynasty nearly as Chinese as the Chinese. More on that in a moment.

At its peak, the Mongol empire spanned the entirety of Asia, plus the Middle East and much of Eastern Europe

GENGHIS KHAN

1162
Born "Temujin" meaning "blacksmith"

1206
Founded Mongol Empire and received name Genghis Khan, meaning "universal ruler"

1227
Died after conquering nearly 12 million square miles of territory

1279
Leads the Mongol Empire to its peak of expansion, twice the size of Caesar's Roman Empire

—that's 12.7 million square miles (33 million square kilometers), or about the size of Africa—all this from an original Mongol population of fewer than 1.5 million people. At any given time, the Great Khan commanded horseback warriors numbering only around 100,000, but his campaigns were legendary, and his strategies emulated by many to follow.

> *"It's not how many breaths you take, but the moments that take your breath away."*
>
> — Genghis Khan

Genghis Khan's detractors point to widespread slaughter of civilians in fallen cities and the ruthlessness of the Mongol horde. Defeated soldiers forced into his army drew the unenviable assignment of "first over the wall" in the next enemy city. But positive accounts do exist: They emphasize his egalitarian outlook, and how he subjected all leaders, including himself, to the same laws. Mongol women played a prominent role at home, as male warriors were gone for long stretches on military campaigns. The Great Khan was known to provide advancement regardless of birthright, and uphold religious freedom for all. Voltaire called him the "king of kings," while Jawaharlal Nehru concluded he was a genius, and the greatest military leader in history.

The death of Genghis Khan remains a mystery. We do know, however, that his story concludes with peasants burying him in an unmarked grave in the countryside, not far from his Mongolian birthplace. They planted trees and trampled the terrain to disguise its location. Those peasants, upon completion of this honorable task, were executed by their attending soldiers. And upon return to the city, those same soldiers were in turn executed by other soldiers, thus ensuring the grave's absolute secrecy. Many have searched, but none has found his final resting place.

EIGHT

What Doesn't Kill You Makes You Stronger

The Mongol conquest of the Chinese heartland

*"The weak fear the strong, the strong fear the violent,
and the violent fear the reckless."*

— Yu Hua

*"Prosperity is not without many fears and distastes;
adversity not without many comforts and hopes."*

— Francis Bacon

YUAN ERA TIMELINE

1271
Kublai Khan declares himself the emperor of the Yuan Dynasty

1280
Astronomer Guo Shoujing creates a calendar that calculates a year as 365.2425 days.

1283
The Catalan Courts ban royal power to unilaterally create legislation

▶ Yuan Dynasty   1271 – 1368   »»

1297
Guan Hanqing, one of the greatest playwrights, creates *Snow in Midsummer*

1298
Marco Polo publishes *Book of the Marvels of the World*, introducing China to Europeans

1320
Dante Alighieri completes *The Divine Comedy*

1299
Osman Gazi (aka "Bone Breaker") establishes the Ottoman Empire

1325
Aztecs found the city of Tenochtitlan

1337
Hundred Years War (1337–1453): Spoiler alert: France wins!

1351
Guo Zixing starts the Red Turban Army to resist Mongol rule

1351
The Black Death devastates Eurasia, killing over 100 million people

Kublai Khan (1215–1294) and the Mongols were the first outsiders to rule all of China in their Yuan Dynasty (1271–1368). Northern tribes—the Xiongnu during the Han Dynasty, the Khitans during the Northern Song, the Jurchens during the Southern Song—all failed. Why? Well, we might say the Chinese had home court advantage, plus a much deeper bench.

China's population dwarfed that of their frontier tribal neighbors. Despite a nomadic, competitive-warrior culture, constant battle-readiness, and the heavy value placed on military prowess, the Mongols were unable to command a decisive advantage. For a tribal leader of horseback warriors, toppling a powerful dynasty would have required constantly adding to a stock of mercenaries. Think of it like a game of Texas Hold 'Em: If you used Kublai's strategy, you'd build up a big stack of chips and then go all in at the perfect moment. But Kublai had pocket aces: he understood Chinese culture, and could sway others into his service, including rebel Chinese generals dissatisfied with the remaining Song leaders and their eroding power.

> *"One can conquer the empire on horseback,*
> *but one cannot govern it on horseback."*
>
> — Kublai Khan

Kublai's multicultural family didn't hurt either. His mother was a Nestorian Christian, and his favorite wife, Chabi, was a Buddhist. His Mongol enemies derided him for his limited military experience, but Kublai compensated for his lack of battlefield machismo with political savvy.

Kublai was an idealist. He harbored ambitions of a shared world alphabet. But he was also a realist: He banned foot binding, calling it archaic, and also eliminated cruel punishments like slow slicing, better known as "death by a thousand cuts." He recognized the challenge of governing as a minority tribe and created equality in power by assigning greater responsibility to Turks, Arabs, and even Europeans within his empire.

TRADITIONAL CHAMBER MUSIC

China's long musical heritage dates back to the Zhou Dynasty (1122–256 BC) when its ceremonial music, called "yayue," was praised by Confucius. There are now hundreds of Chinese instruments, some imported from neighboring states, which modern Chinese orchestras use to create their distinctive sound. Here is a typical five-piece chamber ensemble from Imperial China still common in the China of today.

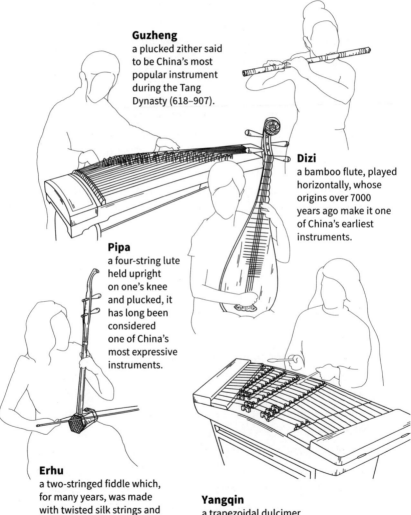

Guzheng
a plucked zither said to be China's most popular instrument during the Tang Dynasty (618–907).

Dizi
a bamboo flute, played horizontally, whose origins over 7000 years ago make it one of China's earliest instruments.

Pipa
a four-string lute held upright on one's knee and plucked, it has long been considered one of China's most expressive instruments.

Erhu
a two-stringed fiddle which, for many years, was made with twisted silk strings and a resonator body covered with python skin.

Yangqin
a trapezoidal dulcimer imported from Persia, it's played by hammering with two lightweight bamboo sticks with rubber tips.

Spinning a Loss into a Win

Despite the Mongols' many cultural distinctions and progressive orientation, China's historians consider the Yuan to be a "Chinese" dynasty, and back their claim with several key points:

1) The Yuan Dynasty government was modeled on Chinese civil society, a conscious decision by Kublai Khan to go with a proven system.
2) The Mongols chose Beijing as their new capital and moved south from Karakorum in Mongolia to reflect the prominence of China within the Empire.
3) Kublai honored his late grandfather Genghis with the Chinese temple name "Taizu," a title traditionally given to the founder of a dynasty. And after Kublai's death, he was given the Chinese temple name "Shizu."
4) Chinese traditions and heritage prevailed across dynasties, since the Mongols made no attempt to assimilate the Han into their culture.

The story begins to sound flimsy, however, when the historic discussion turns to how Chinese culture "civilized" the barbarians, rather than being conquered by a tribe of warriors. Without a doubt, Chinese citizens resented the Mongol presence, and buried their hatred under a veneer of acceptance.

Intellectual Song Dynasty Chinese, excluded from the Yuan government as the lowest of all castes, formed cultural associations and became protectors of the Confucian ideal. Repressed cultures often thrive under oppression, so it's no surprise that the Yuan Dynasty was a golden age for drama. Hundreds of new plays were produced to safeguard Chinese legend. When China sees itself as better than other nations, this viewpoint arises not from a belief in superior race or genetics, but by virtue of its enduring culture.

As it turns out, the Mongol's warrior society was great at winning wars, but terrible at maintaining peace. They coveted the Chinese administrative prowess, but feared mass rebellion, and rationed metal tools so that five Han families were forced to share just one kitchen knife. The Mongol elite further struggled with conflicts between their own adventuresome identity and boring Chinese imperial rituals. Their ways of life were so different that change for either did not prove easy.

Always Look on the Bright Side of Life

As part of the vast Mongol empire, China benefited from renewed communication and trade along the Silk Road. Chinese inventions and ingenuity were exchanged with far-away peoples, including Middle Eastern civilizations that possessed their own traditions of literature, medicine, metallurgy, engineering, and commerce. China flourished under Kublai's reign and remained the leading economy in the world from the 11th to 13th centuries.

One foreigner named Marco Polo is said to have spent 20 years in China, much of it in service to Kublai. Polo traveled the region on recon missions, for the Khan sought to maintain some semblance of control across his vast conquered lands. Not a bad gig for a young Venetian merchant.

Upon his return to Italy, Polo regaled all within earshot with unfathomable tales of immense cities, enlightened rulers, agricultural abundance and widespread paper money. When he was held prisoner during Venice's war with Genoa, he dictated his stories to his cellmate, who happened to be an established Italian romance author. *The Travels of Marco Polo* was published in 1300 and inspired European awareness of the "Far East." It encouraged expanded sea trade and exploration, influencing even the journeys of Christopher Columbus.

The fortunes of Yuan China headed into decline after the death of Kublai, as subsequent Mongol rulers struggled with poor decisions, widespread corruption, and hyperinflation. By the mid 14th century, the bubonic plague had decimated over half of China's population, an epidemic that it's said traveled the trade routes to Europe to become the Black Death.

CHINA'S BIG EIGHT CAPITALS

Anyang 安阳 The discovery of "dragon bones" led to the excavation of this late Shang Dynasty capital known for its bronze age antiquities.

Kaifeng 开封 The capital of Wei during Warring States, Kaifeng later emerged as a powerful commercial center along the Grand Canal, and became the target of numerous attacks by invading northern tribes.

Xi'an 西安 Chang'an (aka Xi'an) was once the largest city in the world, drawing foreigners in along the Silk Road. This ten-time China capital is home to Qin Shihuang's 8,000 battle-ready Terracotta Warriors.

Luoyang 洛阳 A cradle of civilization in the geographic center of China, Luoyang's Longmen Grottoes contain more than 100,000 Buddhist statues.

Nanjing 南京 One of China's Three Furnaces(三大火炉, sān dà huǒ lú), the ancient city of Nanjing was a pivotal location for many rulers up to the start of the Ming era and the capital of the Republic of China under Chiang Kai-shek.

Hangzhou 杭州 First coming to prominence during the Five Dynasties and Ten Kingdoms period, Hangzhou gained popularity in the Song era as a cultural center famous for its refined teas and beautiful scenery.

Zhengzhou 郑州 Another Shang capital, now a fast developing Henan megacity, this five-time capital was also a critical Sui/Tang era transport hub.

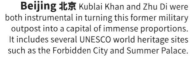

Beijing 北京 Kublai Khan and Zhu Di were both instrumental in turning this former military outpost into a capital of immense proportions. It includes several UNESCO world heritage sites such as the Forbidden City and Summer Palace.

Return of the Han

Driven by the plight of the common people during these desperate times, Zhu Yuanzhang, an overachieving peasant, joined up with and eventually led rebel forces to scatter the Mongols. Zhu founded the Ming Dynasty, and called himself the Hongwu Emperor—not bad for a guy who'd previously been known as a monk and a beggar. And so, in 1368, less than a hundred years after the Mongol encroachment, the Yuan Dynasty was kaput.

The foreign occupation fostered deep introspection and increased confidence in the survivability of Chinese culture. Protecting what was distinctly Chinese became a higher priority than drawing from the outside world was, according to historian Patricia Buckley Ebrey. She notes that China, in this regard, was similar to the Islamic world, in which the Mongol conquests and expansive worldview provoked conservative reactions, rather than interest in the cultures of distant lands.

Beyond the borders of China, the Mongol empire's impact was far more profound. Their concept of "state over church" traveled West and set the stage for the European Age of Enlightenment. Even though Genghis Khan never reached the heart of Europe, he unleashed forces that would forever change the Western mindset.

NINE

This Chapter For Mature Audiences Only

Autonomous Desires in the Ming Dynasty

> "We shall not cease from exploration,
> and the end of all our exploring
> will be to arrive where we started
> and know the place for the first time."
>
> — T.S. Eliot

> "One cannot befriend a man who has no obsessions,
> for such a man lacks deep emotion."
>
> — Zhang Dai

MING ERA TIMELINE

1368
Zhu Yuanzhang founds Ming Dynasty as the Hongwu Emperor

1405
Zheng He leads the first of seven overseas expeditions

1453
Mehmed II conquers Constantinople for the Ottoman Empire

1492
Columbus lands in America

Ming Dynasty 1368–1644

1526
Babur establishes the Mughal empire on the Indian subcontinent

1517
Luther posts the 95 Theses, launching the Protestant Reformation

1522
Magellan's fleet circumnavigates the Earth

1511
Michaelangelo paints the Sistine Chapel's ceiling in the Italian Renaissance

1598
Tang Xianzu finishes the epic play *Peony Pavillion*

1599
Shakespeare pens *Hamlet*

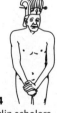

1624
Donglin scholars struggle against the eunuch dictator Wei Zhongxian

1644
Wu Sangui opens the Great Wall's gate at the Shanhai Pass for the Manchu Army to enter

A massive fleet appears on the horizon, featuring treasure ships 480 feet (160 meters) long. Each ship has 12 sails, 4 decks, and a cargo capacitiy of 7,000 tons. Zheng He (郑和, *Zhèng Hé*, 1371–1433), a Muslim eunuch from Yunnan and one of history's greatest sailors, stands on the deck of the main ship, in full command of 317 vessels and a crew of 27,400.

Zheng He's ships bear precious metals, rare silks, and other gifts from the Yongle Emperor, the third emperor of the Ming Dynasty (1368–1644). He offers protection and trade opportunities. Zheng He is also on an international manhunt for a missing emperor (don't laugh, this is serious), thought to be disguised in monk's robes after escaping a fire that engulfed his palace.

The 15th-Century, Open-Door Policy

Let's explore the origins of this remarkable era. Zheng He's first journey, in the year 1405, revived the "aquatic Silk Road" trade route pioneered in the Han Dynasty and later advanced during the Southern Song and Yuan Dynasties. On his seven voyages through 1433, Zheng He covered ports of call from Southeast Asia westward to India, Africa, and the Middle East. These diplomatic missions did as they were expected to do: They expanded China's influence and spread the seeds of Ming culture, 87 years before Columbus reached the Americas and 117 years before Magellan reached the Philippines. They also spawned numerous Zheng He cult followings, including one in the trading enclave of Malacca, where Chinese had earlier settled and intermarried with local Malays to create an entirely new Peranakan, "Straits-born" ethnicity. One historian, Gavin Menzies, even claims that Zheng He beat Columbus to the punch in his controversial book *1421: The Year China Discovered America*, although that idea has been widely disputed. Perhaps it's all relative, since Leif Erikson and the Vikings first reached Newfoundland in the 1100s.

Beyond spreading Ming influence and documenting local cultures, Zheng He's missions also improved cartography and advanced nautical technology. Nanjing shipyards at one point produced upwards of 2,000 ships per year, and the city's foreign

ZHENG HE: THE FLOATING CEO

~27,400 crew members on the first journey in 1405

Personnel Departments

Leadership

Chief and deputy emissaries, supervisors and officials to make decisions on voyage, diplomacy and trading.

Nautical affairs

Captain, helmsman, deck crew for anchors, sails, rowing; weathermen and astrologers, carpenters, blacksmiths.

Military escorts

Soldiers of all ranks from general to private.

Service providers
Foreign affairs (protocol and etiquette experts, communications experts, translators), logistical support (inventory managers, purchasers, cashiers, bookkeepers, secretaries, tailors), and wellbeing (physicians, midwives, barbers).

Spiritual advisors
Daoist masters, monks, and fortune tellers.

language institute minted talented linguists in support of the dynasty's overseas ambitions. China and its navy were leagues ahead of everyone else, poised to usher in a wider era of cultural expansion.

Then it all stopped.

By 1479, the new Ming government had destroyed nearly all the records of these incredible journeys, depriving future generations of their detailed learnings. This set the stage for the "Great Divergence" in the upcoming Qing Dynasty, during which China fell way behind the rapidly industrializing West. But we're getting ahead of ourselves. First, we need to relive a pivotal moment that changed the course of early 15th-century China.

The "Second Founding" of the Ming

It all started with the aforementioned palace fire in the year 1402. Turns out the fire was set by the emperor himself, who fled abdicating the throne to his uncle Zhu Di, fourth son of the aging Ming Dynasty founder, the Hongwu Emperor (朱元璋, *Zhū Yuánzhāng*, 1328–1398). Zhu Di was a headstrong soldier who'd already been passed over for the throne once. The mysterious fire closed the book on Zhu Di's three-year Jingnan Campaign, a civil war between uncle and nephew. And Chinese history proves once again that purging several powerful uncles at the same time can be a tricky proposition.

The Hongwu Emperor brought back the nation's alienated Confucian scholars in 1368 to restore order after the fall of the Mongol Yuan Dynasty. His personal vision was a China that was an agrarian utopia, free of evil influences. He moved the capital to Nanjing and established the Ming as the first dynasty to rule a united China from below the Yangtze River. He also designed China's system of provinces, which is still in place today. Unfortunately, Hongwu had major trust issues and ordered record numbers of executions, reinstating slow slicing and other barbaric tortures for those who dared to criticize him. When he discovered a prime minister plotting against him in 1380, Hongwu beheaded him, then butchered his extended family and social network.

During his reign, Hongwu executed a total of 40,000 people. Such was Hongwu Emperor's difficult reputation that one frustrated scholar arrived for a showdown with the emperor carrying his own coffin! Impressed by this display of bravery, Hongwu spared the scholar's life, but continued his purges of all suspected enemies.

> *"In the morning I punish a few;*
> *by evening others commit the same crime.*
> *I punish those in the evening, and by the next morning,*
> *there are more violations. Although the*
> *corpses of the first lot have not been removed,*
> *already others follow in their path.*
> *The harsher the punishment, the more the violations.*
> *Day and night I cannot rest."*
>
> — Hongwu Emperor

When Zhu Di became the Yongle Emperor (朱棣, *Zhū Dì,* 1360–1424), he reversed most of his late father Hongwu's policies and moved the capital back to Beijing, where Zhu Di had previously ruled as Prince. Yongle reinstated the power of eunuchs, including his trusted ally Zheng He, and used them to offset the Confucians. Yongle then steered Ming China into an era of unprecedented cultural expansion. In a stunning list of accomplishments, Yongle built the Forbidden City, which served as China's imperial palace for the next 500 years, established the Ming Tombs, where he and subsequent Ming rulers were buried, and restored the Grand Canal. These projects transformed Beijing from an overgrown military outpost to an awe-inspiring dynastic capital.

> *"There's a limit to what money can do,*
> *but the power of knowledge is unlimited."*
>
> — Yongle Emperor

Yongle also commissioned the Great Encyclopedia, a massive collection of Chinese history and knowledge, which maxed out at 22,937 chapters and over 370 million words in 11,095 volumes. China once more entered a period of prosperity and stability: Its population doubled and its people began to migrate back North, prompting an expansion of its borders. No longer content to pay off its nomadic neighbors, China kept bringing the fight. Yongle's huge armies defeated the Mongols in five separate battles. He died in 1424 on an arduous campaign in the Gobi Desert.

Neo-Confucian Moral Critiques of Late Ming Decadence

That's a fancy way of introducing the Ming era's breakthrough books—*Romance of the Three Kingdoms*, *Water Margin*, *Journey to the West*, and *Plum in the Golden Vase*—which popularized the use of everyday language in Chinese literature. Professor Andrew Plaks, in his book *Four Masterworks of the Ming Novel*, observes that these fictional works used popular storytelling conventions to elevate societal norms and juxtaposed them against a set of flawed characters in order to raise serious questions about heroism, selfhood, and sexuality. For example, the erotic novel *Plum in the Golden Vase*, often compared with Vatsyayana's *Kama Sutra* from 3rd-century India, but far too risqué to be considered one of China's Four Great Novels (四大名著, *Sì Dà Míng Zhù*), is just as much a cautionary tale about the dangers of excess. A Qing Dynasty critic once quipped that those who regard *Plum in the Golden Vase* as pornographic only read the pornographic parts. So we checked: the book's protagonist, Ximen Qing, had "clouds and rain" with 22 different women. Still, the Ming resurgence of an indulgent courtesan culture, reminiscent of the Tang era, served as a welcome safety valve to arranged marriages and stultifying careers in Confucian officialdom.

Beyond silk, tea, and herbal medicine, ceramics emerged as a valued Chinese export. The archetypal blue and white Ming porcelain vases became all the rage overseas. Wu Renjing, in his

CHINA'S FOUR GREAT NOVELS

China's Four Great Novels (四大名著, *Sì Dà Míng Zhù*) emerged in the 14th to 18th centuries during the Ming and Qing Dynasties, concurrent with the European Renaissance.

The Romance of the Three Kingdoms 三国演义,
Luo Guanzhong (1330–1400)

Chinese literature's first chapter-based novel which draws from the historic power struggle between the Three Kingdoms of Wei, Shu, and Wu (220–280).

Sample line: "The long divided must unite, the long united must divide; thus it has ever been."

Western similarity: *Game of Thrones*

The Water Margin 水浒传,
Shi Nai'an (1296–1370)

A work of controversial authorship based on the true story of the bandit Song Jiang and his 36 rebels in the late years of North Song Dynasty (960–1127).

Sample line: "It's easier to draw a tiger than to sketch its bones. It's easier to know someone's look than the contents of his heart."

Western similarity: *Robin Hood*

Journey to the West 西游记,
Wu Cheng'en (1500–1582)

Most widely told story of the four, it is a fictionalized account of the real pilgrimage to India of the Buddhist monk Xuanzang (602–664).

Sample line: "Heaven and earth were once a chaotic whole, borderless and shapeless, without any beings whatsoever."

Western similarity: *The Lord of the Rings* and *Don Quixote*

Dream of the Red Chamber 红楼梦,
Cao Xueqin (1715–1763)

Semi-autographical work, with over 600 named characters, about the decline of Qing Dynasty (1644–1911) society. Sold over 100 million copies.

Sample line: Pages full of idle words
Penned with hot and bitter tears:
All men call the author fool;
None his secret message hears.

Western similarity: Shakespeare with a dose of Jane Austen

book *History of Chinese Porcelain*, discusses how the porcelain technique reached its apex during the Tang Dynasty, then absorbed artistic influences from Persia and Arabia, giving Ming-era porcelain a glamorous and exotic edge over other ceramics.

The Jesuit missionary Matteo Ricci arrived in 1582. After surveying the culture and grasping the risks of religious evangelism, he opted to establish himself as a learned scholar. Ricci became one of the first Westerners to master reading and writing classical Chinese. He even compiled his own Chinese phonetic dictionaries complete with tone marks, an early precursor to modern Pinyin. His efforts to learn the language won him many Christian converts. He also leveraged Confucian terms to explain Catholic Church liturgy, in a replay of how Daoism was enlisted to diffuse Buddhist precepts during the Tang era. Ricci later advised the Wanli Emperor, and was the first westerner to be admitted into the Forbidden City. When Ricci died, he was allowed to be buried in Beijing, instead of in the trading outpost of Macau, where most Westerners were buried.

How Can I Miss You If You Won't Go Away?

The Wanli Emperor (朱翊钧, *Zhū Yìjūn,* 1563–1620) was the thirteenth and longest reigning Ming emperor, ruling for 48 years during the decline of the dynasty. Wanli is most remembered for his conspicuous abandonment of duty and refusing to meet with his ministers for over 20 years. Before we throw rotten tomatoes at him for precipitating the fall of the Ming Dynasty, let's hear Wanli's side of the story, as he had some good reasons for boycotting his ministers.

Wanli's reign started well. He was just a boy of ten, after all, relying on his talented Senior Grand Secretary, Zhang Juzheng, to deliver reforms and economic development to the people. He waged wars with the Mongols and Japan, proving himself highly competent. He tolerated decades of moralistic one-upmanship among his Confucian court officials, only to have them block his choice of successor. Why couldn't they remember all his many other competent decisions? And what was he supposed to tell his favorite concubine, the mother of his choice for crown prince?

The Hongwu Emperor would have slaughtered them all.

But Wanli caved in and agreed to the officials' choice for successor. Big loss of face. He then sequestered himself in the Forbidden City and refused to speak directly to any of his advisors for the next two decades. Officials had to bribe a member of his eunuch entourage just to have messages delivered to him, behavior reflective of the overall Ming decline. Similar to early 17th century Japan, which closed its doors to Western merchants and missionaries, China became increasingly weak and isolationist, setting the stage for the upcoming Manchu takeover.

> *"I'm scared of the Censors because
> they challenge me all the time."*
>
> — Wanli Emperor

In the bitter end of the Ming Dynasty, 24 years after the death of Wanli, the Chongzhen Emperor drew his sword, slew his own family, then hanged himself from a tree outside the Forbidden City. Beijing fell to a rebel army led by Li Zicheng, one of several powerful Chinese warlords competing to take control. Turncoat Ming general Wu Sangui then sided with the Manchu enemy against Li Zicheng, whom it's said stole Wu's woman. Wu Sangui opened the Great Wall gate at the Shanhai Pass, allowing the Manchu army to enter China.

Many historians have concluded that the Ming failed to live up to its potential. Emperors and their Confucian advisors were all well aware of the best leadership practices of China's most successful dynasties, yet much of the Ming was mired in factionalism and political infighting, and nursing a dysfunctional financial structure. Meanwhile, the sharpest intellectual minds of its age were sidetracked by esoteric ethical debates, rather than uniting on the practical matter of how society can benefit its people. Ray Huang, who studies the Ming era, observes, "This highly stylized society wherein the roles of individuals were thoroughly restricted by a body of simple yet ill-defined moral

THE FORBIDDEN CITY

Completed in the year 1420, this home to 24 Ming and Qing Dynasty emperors is among the world's most-visited tourist attractions, seeing 15 million tourists per year.

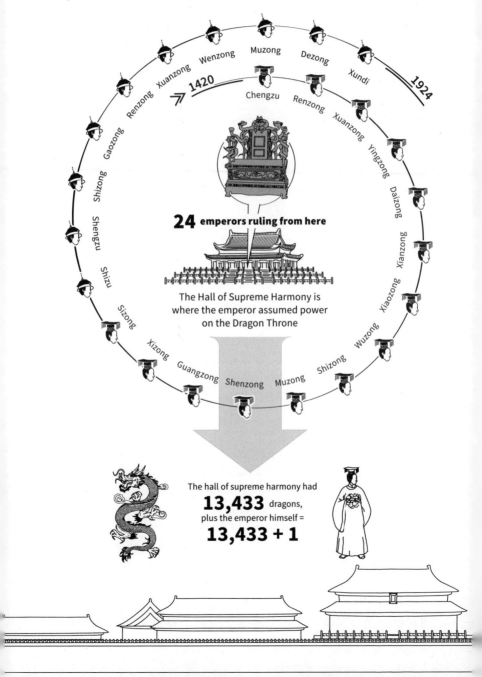

132-ton rocks sledded on ice from quarries for

43 miles (70 kilometers)

980 buildings with **8,707** rooms

At the height of Ming Dynasty, there were over **100,000** eunuchs in service

The Ming Dynasty imperial harem had **9,000** handmaidens and concubines

The chosen ones head the East and West wings of the back court, close to the emperor's bedroom.

Emperors work hard and play hard

① The inner court for private life

② The outer court for political obligations

723,633m² total area

753m × 961m

An official's morning routine

Midnight
① Heading out to the Forbidden City

3:00 a.m
② Waiting outside the meridian gate

Dawn
③ Morning meeting with the emperor

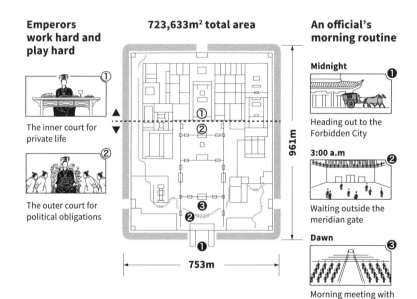

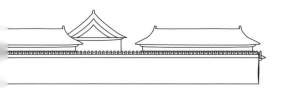

precepts, the empire was seriously hampered in its development, regardless of the noble intention behind those precepts." The official History of Ming singles out the slacking Wanli Emperor as instigator of the dynasty's torturous decline. The Hongwu Emperor had a vision of an agrarian utopia, and the Yongle Emperor achieved broad trade and cultural outreach, but this dynasty's destiny seems unfulfilled.

TEN

Mind Your P's and Queues

The Qing Dynasty's potent peaks and quarrelsome quagmires

"The wealthy vie with each other in splendor and display, while the poor squeeze each other to death."

— Gong Zizhen

"Everything one does in life, even love, occurs in an express train racing toward death. To smoke opium is to get out of the train while it is still moving. It is to concern oneself with something other than life or death."

— Jean Cocteau

QING ERA TIMELINE

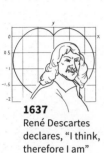

1637
René Descartes declares, "I think, therefore I am"

1687
Issac Newton formulates the Laws of Motion

1698
Peter the Great implements sweeping reforms to modernize Russia

1776
U.S. Founding Fathers sign the *Declaration of Independence*

▶ Qing Dynasty 1644 – 1911 ⟫

1848
Karl Marx publishes *The Communist Manifesto*

1839
Pope Gregory XVI issues the Papal Bull condemning slavery

1793
Marie Antoinette beheaded during the French Revolution

1792
Cao Xueqin's *Dream of Red Mansions* is published

1894
Sun Yat-sen establishes the Revive China Society

1898
Cixi blocks Guangxu Emperor's major reforms

1905
Emperor abolishes the Civil Service Exam after 1300 years

1912
Yuan Shikai assumes power, marking the end of the Qing Dynasty

The time was ripe for a new kind of leadership. The Manchus, from their homeland northeast of the Great Wall, were ready to deliver it.

Unlike the nomadic Mongols, the Manchus were a Tungusic people, whose society was based on farming, hunting, and fishing. The Manchus considered themselves descendants of the Jurchens, who ran the Jin Dynasty (1115–1234) in northern China in parallel with the Southern Song Dynasty. And since their template of governance was modeled on the Chinese system, the Manchus saw it as a natural step to now rule the whole of China in their Qing Dynasty (1644–1911).

When the Manchus arrived to conquer China, they were outnumbered a hundred to one by the Han people. It took them nearly forty years to consolidate control over the entire country, a staggering accomplishment made possible only by the vast number of anti-Ming Chinese and Mongols who rallied to support them. The Manchu Eight Banners military comprised only 16% Manchu soldiers, with 76% Chinese and 8% Mongols forming the bulk of the forces. Care to venture a guess which ones had to trudge through the toughest terrain and ferret out the fiercest Ming holdouts? In contrast to the Confucian view on soldiers as lower class citizens, the Manchus held their military officers in high esteem and offered their loyal generals career paths into prestigious positions: For instance the Yunnan regional governorship was granted to Wu Sangui for opening the gate for the Manchu army.

There's no question that the Manchu "Aisin Gioro" family saw themselves as rulers of a "Chinese dynasty" in pursuit of a multiethnic, harmonious society. And in a clever move, they selected the water element Qing (清, *qīng,* lit. "pure") to extinguish the fire element Ming (明, *míng,* lit. "bright") and establish cultural continuity in the new dynasty.

Perhaps it's human nature that induces us to take the good times for granted and assume they'll go on forever. The first half of the Qing Dynasty witnessed an exceptional period of prosperity and power—Patricia Buckley Ebrey refers to it as a high point of traditional Chinese civilization—followed by a second half plagued by unimaginative thinking and, for the first time in China's history, domination by more advanced overseas nations.

Queues, Qipaos, and Qianlong

The early succession of Manchu emperors (Kangxi, Yongzheng, and Qianlong) ruled China for an incredible stretch of stability from 1684 to 1799. They pushed China's territorial footprint well beyond the glory days of the Tang Dynasty. For the most part, these guys were early-rising, hard-working autocrats who listened to their ministers, a welcome departure from the Ming's dysfunctional "eunuchs vs. officials" style of governance. The Qing rulers created an effective parallel administration: Manchus monitored Han Chinese, who were in turn recruited to positions of authority by the imperial examination system.

THE QIPAO: FROM CLASSIC TO MODERN

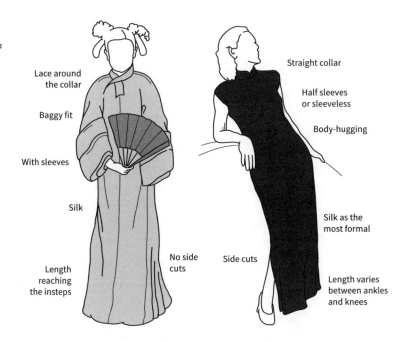

Originated in the Qing Dynasty as a one-piece dress for Manchu women

Modernized in Shanghai and remains popular among fashionistas

The Qing era's first flash point arose from a highly contentious disagreement over, of all things, hairstyles. The Queue Order of 1645 forced all Chinese males to shave bald in front and grow a rat-tail queue in the back, mirroring the Manchus, so that everyone could be easily identified as friend or foe. The Han Chinese detested this edict, which they explained in sardonic terms: "To keep your hair, you lose your head; to keep your head, you cut your hair." The Chinese believed that hair, like the rest of one's body, was a precious gift from one's parents, so this act read as a betrayal of one's own ancestors. Indeed, some chose having their heads lopped off rather than comply.

The prolific Kangxi Emperor (Aisin-Gioro hiowan yei, 1654–1722) ruled for 61 years, setting the record for longest reign of any emperor in Chinese history (big round of applause, please!). He took the stage as the fourth Qing emperor at age eight, dominated by four previously appointed regents with their own political agendas. At age 16, he pushed them aside and took over. Kangxi then suppressed rebellions and battled the Russians, who had begun to encroach on the China's borders. He also addressed the needs of peasants through reform of the forced labor system and instituted tax collection based on land ownership and ability to pay.

> "Among those who realize the value of self-reflection, many will become high achievers."
>
> — Kangxi Emperor

Kangxi was a nerd at heart. He spent most of his spare time learning mathematics, geology, medicine, music, astronomy, and meteorology. He studied with Jesuit missionaries, whom he welcomed as court advisors, while also mastering calligraphy and the Confucian classics. His pet project was to survey the Chinese empire, and he carted around his own equipment to create an impressive collection of topographical maps. Records show that Kangxi avoided the sensual overindulgence to which other emperors fell prey. Instead, his legacy was to curate a vast collection of books, including the eponymous Kangxi Dictionary, which contains over 47,000 Chinese characters. For centuries, it was the definitive Chinese dictionary.

Kangxi's favorite grandson, soon to rule as the Qianlong Emperor, was his heir apparent from an early age. Providence seemed to aid Qianlong at every turn. Some historians have surmised that Kangxi, on his deathbed, chose Qianlong's father (the short-reigned Yongzheng Emperor) from among the seven competing crown princes in hopes that Qianlong would quickly succeed him. And if indeed that was his intention, it worked.

Someday All This Will Be Yours

The Qianlong Emperor (Aisin-Gioro hala i Hung-Li, 1711–1799) assumed command at age 24. He overflowed with confidence, was well versed in martial arts, and armed with a shrewdness honed by listening in on the strategy meetings of both his father and grandfather. Qianlong thought big. He talked big. And he backed it up with action.

Qianlong immediately quelled the Miao Rebellions in southwest China, then led expansion campaigns into Xinjiang, Tibet, and Mongolia. He nearly doubled the size of the empire. Unsuccessful attempts to push into Burma and Vietnam under the pretext of enforcing regional order, plus a dwindling treasury, forced Qianlong to dial back his ambitions. Critics have accused Qianlong of widespread massacres, that he created peace and prosperity based on copious bloodshed.

Qianlong also preserved China's cultural heritage and curated large collections of paintings, bronzes, and jades for the glory of the Qing, perhaps recalling the legacy of Song Huizong, the artist emperor. Qianlong was a prolific writer who authored 43,630 poems over his lifetime, some in other languages. That's 1.7 new poems every day of his adult life. He went on to spearhead the compilation of 3,500 literary works from past dynasties by employing 15,000 scribes to amass the Four Treasuries Complete Collection. But in what had become a familiar pattern of Chinese history revisionism from Qin Shihuang, to Song Huizong, to

Kublai Khan, Qianlong purged the scrolls of any passage that reflected anti-Manchu sentiment. Large numbers of offending volumes, in particular, those from the Ming era, were burned during his literary inquisition. Keep in mind that, during this era, barely 1% of Chinese could read or write. The common people went about their day with no idea their descendants were to be cheated out of a balanced history.

> *"We possess all things.*
> *I set no value on objects strange or ingenious,*
> *and have no use for your country's [Britain's] manufactures."*
>
> — Qianlong Emperor

China controlled one-third of the world's wealth in the 18th century, and its population during the Qianlong era more than doubled to over 300 million people. The simmering masses, however, remained dirt poor. When Qianlong rebuked Britain's trade offer, he did so out of concern for how increased trade and open borders might destabilize Manchu rule.

After Qianlong's death, subsequent Qing emperors continued the struggle to find solutions to the crushing cycle of poverty and prevent the outbreak of rebellion. Meanwhile, Han Chinese were increasingly mobile. Chinese merchants of Hokkien, Hakka, and Teochew ethnicities found sanctuary in the ports of Southeast Asian and built regional trading networks. The most successful among them became "Lords of the Rim," a term coined by author Sterling Seagrave. The Manchu, like the Ming rulers before them, banned migration, fearing that overseas Chinese colonies would become hotbeds of seditious conspiracy. Large numbers of people, however, ignored the threat of beheading and moved anyway.

CHINESE MASS MIGRATIONS

After his Manchu Army wiped out the nomadic Dzungars in the grasslands of northern Xinjiang, Emperor Qianlong ordered Han, Hui, and other peoples to repopulate the area, including the new city of Urumqi.

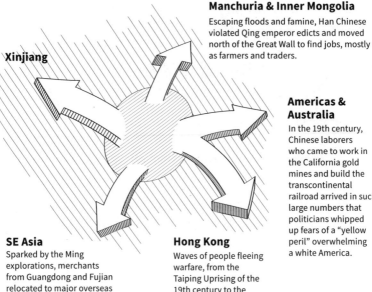

Xinjiang

Manchuria & Inner Mongolia
Escaping floods and famine, Han Chinese violated Qing emperor edicts and moved north of the Great Wall to find jobs, mostly as farmers and traders.

Americas & Australia
In the 19th century, Chinese laborers who came to work in the California gold mines and build the transcontinental railroad arrived in such large numbers that politicians whipped up fears of a "yellow peril" overwhelming a white America.

SE Asia
Sparked by the Ming explorations, merchants from Guangdong and Fujian relocated to major overseas ports and cultivated regional trading networks. In the 19th century, the poorest Chinese and Indians were sold into indentured servitude as coolies and shipped overseas.

Hong Kong
Waves of people fleeing warfare, from the Taiping Uprising of the 19th century to the Japanese invasion and Communist/Nationalist conflicts of the 20th century, crossed the border into this then-British colony.

What Do You Mean You Don't Want Our Drugs Anymore?

The First Opium War of 1840–42 started as a trade disagreement turned ugly and ended in the Treaty of Nanjing. If you haven't heard of this treaty, perhaps you'll remember the document by its full name: "The Treaty of Peace, Friendship, and Commerce between Her Majesty the Queen of Great Britain and Ireland and the Emperor of China." There's no mention of the Brits singing "For He's A Jolly Good Fellow" after the Qing diplomats signed it at gunpoint.

The Chinese were already smoking plenty of opium before the 19th century when Britain ratcheted up its imports into China, though it was mainly for medicinal use. Recreational smoking by people to take the edge off laborious or monotonous lives expanded in contravention to both law and Confucian social mores. More and more people became addicted. Naturally the emperor and his ministers reacted with alarm to this flouting of the rules, and the rapid outflow of silver from their treasury.

The British struggled with a massive trade imbalance of their own due to high demands for tea, silk, and porcelain. To offset this imbalance, and overcome the import bottleneck in Guangzhou, William Jardine, commercial agent for the Honourable East India Company (yes, that's its full name), ramped up shipments of their more potent opium from India into China. The East India Company (EIC) dominated large sections of India with its own private armies and, at one point in time, controlled half the world's trade. The total volume of opium entering China from the EIC and others went from 1,000 chests in 1767 up to 40,000 chests in 1838, a fortyfold increase.

Enough was enough. The emperor empowered Lin Zexu (林则徐, *Lín Zéxú,* 1785–1850), an incorruptible foreign affairs commissioner, to solve the problem. Lin tried his best, even offering to swap Chinese tea for the smuggled drugs. At his peak of frustration, Lin wrote a letter to Queen Victoria: "Suppose there were people from another country who carried opium for sale to England and seduced your people into buying and smoking it; certainly your honorable ruler would deeply hate it and be bitterly aroused. If you could get rid of all the opium plants and turn the land to growing grains, and lay heavy punishment for whomever dared to plant opium, that would benefit us all, and the heavens would bless you with longevity and many offspring." In the end, Lin destroyed as much opium as he could and arrested the wrongdoers.

In response to Lin Zexu's blatant trade interference, Jardine sailed home to Great Britain and lobbied for war. This wasn't a bright spot in the history of capitalism, although many British

CHINA'S OPIUM OBSESSION

Fascination
The Sumerians called poppies the "joy plant" and cultivated them in Mesopotamia over five thousand years ago, but it wasn't until 600 that Arab traders first brought opium to China. Doctors in many cultures prescribed opium — all taken orally — to patients for a variety of ailments. Chinese recreational use didn't start until the 15th century. Recognizing its dangers, the Yongzheng Emperor outlawed opium in 1729.

Addiction
The opium pipe, aka the "dream stick," introduced the common Chinese to a rapid and highly-addictive delivery method. Despite heavy penalties against its use, opium imports rose from only 1,000 chests per year under the Qianlong Emperor (1736–1796) to 30,000 chests per year under the Daoguang Emperor (1821–1850). China was forced to legalize opium in 1860 after its defeat in the Second Opium War. By 1906, China was producing 85 percent of the world's opium and 27 percent of its adult male population were regular users.

Eradication
Starting in the 1890s, foreign missionaries lobbied to end the opium trade and ban its use in China. Opium farming in China peaked in the 1930s. Mao's government executed all the dealers and substituted other crops in the 1950s. Production then moved south into Myanmar, Laos, and Thailand (aka The Golden Triangle).

disagreed with the war. And it's unlikely the Queen ever saw Lin's heartfelt letter. Still, the crown sided with the EIC and declared war on China.

After a series of one-sided battles along the coast, China signed the first of numerous unequal settlements. The Treaty of Nanjing opened five treaty ports including Shanghai, demanded reparation payments from China, and opened the door to missionaries. The British also ended up in possession of a barren island known as Hong Kong. This shocking military defeat woke China to the reality that it had already fallen behind Western development (the so-called "Great Divergence") and marked the beginning of China's Century of Humiliation.

Qing authorities were soon to have a far worse catastrophe on their hands. In the southwestern province of Guangxi, a militant evangelist named Hong Xiuquan (洪秀全, *Hóng Xiùquán,* 1814–1864), who believed himself to be the son of God and younger brother of Jesus Christ, attracted upwards of 50,000 followers in Hunan province alone into his "Heavenly Kingdom of Transcendent Peace." Tensions rose between the authorities and the sect; it didn't help that Hong was destroying Confucian and Buddhist relics in his mission to rid the world of demon worship. Hong's followers routed government forces and beheaded its Manchu commander. The authorities labeled them the "hair traitors" (发贼, *fà zéi*) because they refused to shave or wear the queue.

Failed attempts to suppress this so-called Long Hair Movement increased its grassroots support and instigated the Taiping Rebellion, which lasted from 1850 to 1864 and took the lives of over 50 million people. Many died from famine and disease. It was the bloodiest civil war in history, worse than the brutal American Civil War fought on the other side of the planet. Hong's remarkable Sinicized Christianity might have succeeded, had it not alienated foreign missionaries and antagonized the Confucian elite necessary to create a viable replacement for the faltering Qing government.

In 1860, British and French forces looted then burned down the Old Summer Palace in Beijing in retaliation for the torture and killing of a team of envoys sent to negotiate an end to the Second

Opium War. The palace featured hundreds of buildings with stunning architectural designs from across the empire and fairytale gardens of unimaginable beauty. Commissioned by Kangxi and finished by Qianlong over a century later, the Palace grounds were almost three times the size of the Forbidden City and eight times the size of the Vatican City. French dramatist Victor Hugo lamented the destruction of the Old Summer Palace: "This wonder has disappeared...We Europeans are the civilized ones, and for us, the Chinese are the barbarians. This is what civilization has done to the barbarian."

Ruling from Behind the Curtain

One of the most controversial women in history, the Empress Dowager Cixi (1835–1908) manipulated the succession of Qing emperors to gain control of the nation. Nobody expected this ordinary girl, born into a humble Manchu family, to become the most powerful person in China for an incredible 47 years, from 1861 to her death in 1908. Cixi was at times China's most ardent benefactor, and its biggest impediment to progress.

Cixi was an intelligent girl who went against social norms and read books during an age of female illiteracy. At age 16, in keeping with tradition, Cixi was paraded past Emperor Xianfeng with droves of other young women, all Manchu or Mongol. (Intermarriage with the Han was forbidden.) She was chosen as a low-ranking concubine. To survive as a nobody in the cutthroat harem of an imperial emperor, Cixi knew she needed the potent combination of beautiful looks, political savvy, and the ability to produce an heir to the throne. Her big break came when she gave birth to Xianfeng's first surviving son and became the emperor's most prized consort, second only to the empress. Upon the emperor's death, Cixi executed a coup d'état and began to advise her young son, the newly-installed Emperor Tongzhi, from behind a curtain near his throne.

Cixi accomplished numerous things that her predecessors could not: She was instrumental in saving the Qing Dynasty from the Taiping Rebellion. She also improved female education and issued an edict to end foot-binding. Although she loathed Western ways, Cixi endorsed China's "self-strengthening" movement, designed to

CIXI CLIMBS THE RANKS OF THE CONCUBINE SYSTEM

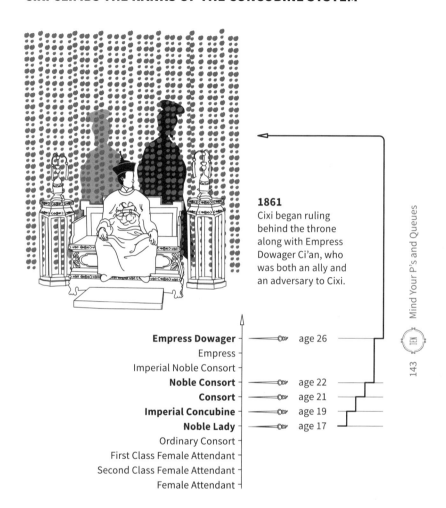

1861
Cixi began ruling behind the throne along with Empress Dowager Ci'an, who was both an ally and an adversary to Cixi.

co-opt the best economic and military practices of the West and yet preserve superior Chinese values.

Cixi's undoing was her inability to break free of the conservative faction of Manchu reactionaries, who continued to put the self-interests of the Qing court ahead of the Chinese nation. With her appointment of her nephew in 1887 as the Guangxu Emperor, much to everyone's relief, Cixi entered "retirement." In reality, with China facing one crisis after another, Cixi never relinquished control.

As China floundered, Japan surged ahead. American Commodore Matthew Perry's "gunboat diplomacy" back in 1852 had prompted Japan's Meiji Restoration era of rapid modernization. Japan then shocked everyone with its easy victory over China in the First Sino-Japanese War (1894–1895) to become the region's dominant power. Japan captured Korea and was ceded Taiwan. Russia and Germany leapt into the fray, while Britain, France, and Japan scrambled for more Chinese concessions. The Guangxu emperor attempted positive change in 1898 with the Hundred Days Reform, only to bump up against Cixi: She came out of retirement to execute his reform-minded officials and reclaim control.

> *"Britain is one of the world's most powerful countries.*
> *But it doesn't owe it all to Queen Victoria herself.*
> *The Parliament was helpful and supportive ...*
> *but look at me who has to manage 400 million people.*
> *I'm the one who has to decide everything.*
> *My military ministers are corrupt cowards.*
> *And the Emperor doesn't know a thing."*
>
> — Empress Dowager Cixi

Into this fomentation came a xenophobic, martial arts-inspired peasant movement called the Fists of United Righteousness or The Boxers. Frustrated by the China's impotence in the face of foreign aggression, and distressed by Christian proselytizing and favoritism in Shandong province, the home of Confucius, the Boxers set out to cleanse the nation of foreigners by fire and blood. The Boxers were a strange sight to behold. Clad in red turbans and leather boots, they sang and shouted invocations in the belief that they could become immune to weapons and bullets. The Qing court's reluctance to suppress the uprising—as ugly as things had become, Cixi clung to the desperate hope the Boxers might succeed—prompted Western governments to view China as a failed state. An Eight-Nation Alliance army (the main European powers, plus Russia, Japan, and the U.S.) streamed into Beijing to save their desperate nationals, trapped under seige. In the end, China was forced to sign yet another mortifying treaty.

By the time Cixi died in 1908, the much-vaunted Chinese cultural superiority honed by Confucian intellectuals over the centuries had suffered a complete collapse of confidence. Historians would later overlook Cixi's early accomplishments to blame her for the decline and fall of the Qing.

Prime Ministers, Presidents, and Puyi

As fate would have it, the final role in an astounding procession of 557 emperors would be played by an innocent young boy named Puyi (溥仪, *Pǔyí,* 1906–1967), who also answered to the name Henry. Cixi, on her deathbed, chose Puyi to begin his rein as the Xuantong Emperor at age 2 years and 10 months. Puyi ruled for just three years during the tumultuous close of China's two thousand plus year imperial era, and inspired the 1987 film *The Last Emperor* by Bernardo Bertolucci.

> *"Oh, how magical it will be to have winter come every year."*
>
> — Emperor Puyi

It all happened so fast. Puyi was thrust into the limelight, and robbed of his childhood. He was pushed into loveless marriages by Manchu royalty, and eventually forced to abdicate by the Nationalists after the 1911 Xinhai Revolution. Decades later the imperialist Japanese put him on the throne as a puppet emperor in their Manchukuo state in China's northeast. When the Communists seized power, they imprisoned him for socialist reeducation. Puyi did not find peace until the age of 54, when he became a common gardener in the Beijing Botanical Garden.

PEKING OPERA

Cixi and the Qing imperial court adored Peking Opera, an art form which originated in the 19th century by combining elements of local Chinese folk operas.

Sheng 生
Male characters, leading roles with subtypes, e.g. aged (laosheng), young and handsome (xiaosheng), martial skills (wusheng)

Jing 净
Supporting male characters with painted faces (over a thousand variations), strong personalities, and exaggerated gestures. Face color and design symbolism reveal their inner nature.

Dan 旦
Female characters, major roles with subtypes, e.g. gentle and quiet (qingyi), beautiful (huadan), aged (laodan)

Chou 丑
Comic characters, entertaining secondary roles with more dialog than singing, may also involve improv and martial arts skills.

Males playing females (and vice versa)

From the beginning of their popularity in the Yuan Dynasty until three hundred years later in the Qing Dynasty, all stage roles were played by male performers. That's why female roles were played by male artists. Stages opened to female artists in the late Qing, though for many years, males and females could not perform together. This led to all-female opera casts covering the male characters. In recent times, female-played male roles and male-played female roles have shared the same stage.

Mei Lanfang (1894–1961)
An iconic Peking Opera artist, Mei's most memorable "Dan" role was Beauty Yu in *Farewell My Concubine*.

Meng Xiaodong (1908–1977)
One of the most successful female "Sheng" artists remembered for her roles playing dignified older men.

Peking Opera audience tips

The audience at a Peking Opera is advised to respond with spontaneity and passion to the action on stage. Think of it as cheering for the fast-changing action of a sports match, rather than a polite round of applause held until the end of a movement by a symphony orchestra.

For example, when an artist makes a dramatic movement or a powerful vocal performance, the audience should clap or shout "hao!" (i.e. well-done or bravo!) at the top of their lungs. A quiet audience may actually upset the artists and compromise the momentum of the show.

The more excited the audience, the better the show!

ELEVEN

Enter the Fashion Icons

Revolutionaries who ignited a nation

"My own attitude is that we must unreservedly accept this modern civilization of the West because we need it to solve our most pressing problems, the problems of poverty, ignorance, disease, and corruption."

— Hu Shi

"A handful of might is better than a bagful of right."

— Max Stirner

20TH CENTURY TIMELINE

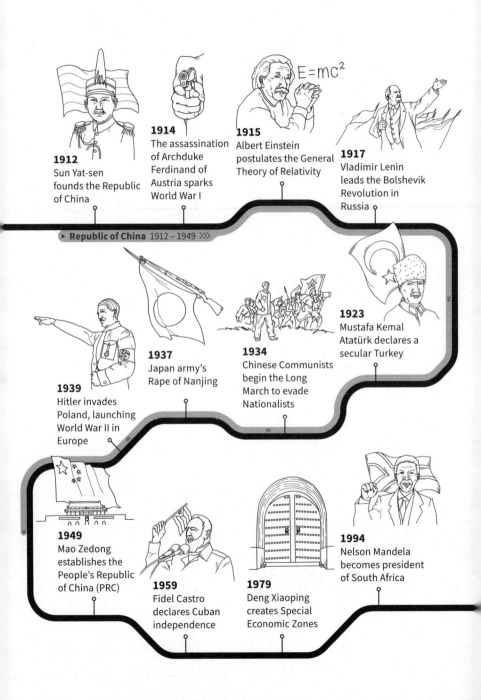

The scene: Tiananmen Square. Three thousand Beijing students shout accusations and patriotic slogans at their backward government. The scene turns ugly.

Protestors set fire to a cabinet minister's home. Police intervene to disperse the mob and arrest 1,150 protesters, turning parts of Beijing University into a makeshift jail. The Beijing government doesn't know it's already too late to contain the upswell of popular discontent. Students go on strike in other cities, and soon, everyone has heard the rallying cry. They demand action. China's brightest young minds are saying, "We're not going to take it anymore."

The date? May 4, 1919: The start of the May Fourth Movement and the event many historians point to as the birth of modern China.

Do the Right Thing

It all started with bad news out of France. The Treaty of Versailles, signed by victorious Western powers at the completion of the First World War, should have returned German concessions in Shandong Province to their rightful owner, China. Instead, the treaty gave them to China's usurping occupier, Japan, which was already in control of Manchuria and strategizing ways to swallow the entire country. What's worse, China's own northern warlord government (soon to be ousted) was complicit in the deal: they'd taken Japanese "loans" in exchange for staying quiet. Some thanks for China, who sent 140,000 laborers to France in support of the Allied war effort.

It was a true wake-up call. Much of the Nationalist intellectual discussion was focused on the superiority of Western science and democracy. Everything Chinese was under scrutiny, especially its calcified Confucianism and passive acceptance of feudal traditions. Lu Xun, a well-known man of letters, determined to launch a literary movement which author Jonathan Spence recognizes as seeking "to bring out the reserves of willpower latent in the Chinese people, to imbue his countrymen with the heroic and demonic strength to change their destiny." Scholar Yan Fu criticized the Chinese "Way of the Sages" and argued for a

Western form of government to free the energy of the individual towards collective goals. He once commented that only 30 percent of China's troubles were caused by foreigners; the rest were her own fault and could be remedied by her own actions. May Fourth confirmed the notion that China had to solve its own problems, and intensified the debate on how to repurpose foreign political ideals to help China become a powerful and progressive nation.

LU XUN: DOCTOR OF CLEAR THINKING

Author, translator, editor, and poet, Lu Xun (鲁迅, Lǔ Xùn, 1881–1936) is said to have quit Western medical school in Japan after seeing the disturbing image of a Japanese soldier about to behead a Chinese spy, surrounded by a crowd of apathetic Chinese onlookers.

"Lies written in ink can never disguise facts written in blood."

"A bad memory is an advantage to its owner but injurious to his descendants. The ability to forget the past enables people to free themselves gradually from the pain they once suffered; but it also makes them repeat the mistakes of their predecessors."

"Those who once had power want to go back to the past. Those in power now want to remain as they are. Those who have not yet had power want reforms. This is a general rule."

"There are no paths in life. When many people start walking paths appear."

"Chinese like to choose what's in the middle. For example, if a room is too dark and a window needs to be opened, they'll disagree, but if you suggest to take the roof off, then they'd rather have the window open."

Lǔ Xùn

鲁 迅

The Republic's Founding Father

Let's back up for a moment to the year 1911, when China's revolutionaries appointed Sun Yat-sen (孙中山, *Sūn Zhōngshān*, 1866–1925) as the provisional president of their new Republic. Sun had struggled for decades in the cause of reform: He petitioned the Qing court to modernize the nation — rejected. He led ten uprisings against the Qing — all failed. He spent years in exile to avoid capture. When the Xinhai Revolution of 1911 broke the Qing stranglehold on power and ended over two thousand years of imperial rule, Sun was in the United States. Nonetheless, his fellow revolutionaries recognized him as their resilient and highly-vocal leader.

Sun's signature piece was his "Three Principles of the People," first articulated while speaking in Brussels in 1905. Here is his much-acclaimed philosophy in a nutshell:

1) Nationalism (民族主义, *Mínzú Zhǔyì*) — advance an anti-imperialist spirit to unite all the ethnic groups of China and escape foreign domination.

2) Democracy (民权主义, *Mínquán Zhǔyì*) — power to the people, which to Sun and others implied a Western-style constitutional government adapted to China, i.e. not necessarily one-person, one-vote open elections.

3) People's welfare (民生主义, *Mínshēng Zhǔyì*) — provide for China's citizens, through tax reform and much-improved government support, in contrast to pure capitalism or pure socialism.

The frantic Manchu Qing court still had one card up its sleeve. They persuaded the crafty General Yuan Shikai (袁世凯, *Yuán Shìkǎi*, 1859–1916), still in charge of the country's most powerful army, to suppress the Republican rebellion. Yuan instead brokered a deal with the revolutionaries to kick out Emperor Puyi and take over the role of President. But this was also just a ploy. Yuan betrayed his revolutionary allies and made a hasty U-turn to dissolve their fledgling parliament, assassinate a political opponent, reinstitute Confucianism, revive the monarchy, and, get this, become its new emperor. General Yuan justified his imperious behavior with the oft-heard claim that the ignorant Chinese masses were accustomed to an autocratic ruler. Maintaining stability, he said, was always number one.

Yuan's plan flopped. He died three months later.

The army scattered, and oh no, not again, it was back to warlords and chaos. The republican spirit of reform was far from dead, however. All the big name revolutionaries, at least for now, were aligned under the Nationalist banner: Sun Yat-sen; his protégé, Chiang Kai-shek; reformers Kang Youwei and Liang Qichao; Chinese Communist Party (CCP) founders Chen Duxiu and Li Dazhao; and the lesser-known intellectuals, Zhou Enlai, Deng Xiaoping, and Mao Zedong. These were heady days. *New Youth Magazine* published socialist musings and China's new populist vernacular was on the rise. Women's rights were at the forefront and there was a major push to eliminate bound feet and forced marriages, and even allow divorce. Believe it or not, women were still not supposed to dine with men at the same table!

Sun wisely insisted on alignment between Nationalists and Communists towards the common goal of establishing a modern Chinese nation. Fresh off the Bolshevik Revolution, Vladimir Lenin was more than happy to supply a thousand Communist International advisers (advocating a world communist revolution) to help China overthrow its warlords, and offset the growing influence of Russia's arch-enemy Japan. But there wouldn't be a full socialist revolt in China, since the depressed and exploited urban proletariat didn't exactly exist. Communism in China still had a long road ahead.

THE GOLDEN AGE OF SHANGHAI

"Shanghai was where the modern world began, where the seeds of Chinese capitalism first came to flower. It was a foretaste of what other Asian cities would be like in the next generation. The city pulsed with physical and mental vigor. By the 1920s it had emerged from a provincial sort of urbanity into true cosmopolitanism."
– Lynn Pan

Shanghai (上海, *Shànghǎi*, "on the sea") was really three cities in one: the walled Chinese city, the French Concession, and the International Settlement, which had its own racetrack for Mongolian horses.
In 1921, the CCP held its first covert meeting in a deserted school in the French Concession.

A flowering of liberal and reformist thought in the late 1920s turned Shanghai into the literary and intellectual capital of China. Ballroom dancing became the rage, with the opening of the Paramount nightclub in 1933 and a Russian jazz orchestra playing nightly at the Majestic Theater. China's film industry became an ideological battleground between the Nationalists and Communists. By 1949 immigrants swelled Shanghai's population to over five million. Today 24 million people live in the city.

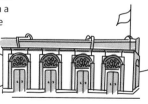

> "Comparing human and physical properties, we must admit that it's easier to direct matter than man. For this reason, science has advanced by leaps and bounds, and the means of controlling nature have been nearly perfected, and placed at our disposal. We can build machines to fly in, machines to travel in under water. Human affairs, however, are exceedingly complicated."
>
> — Sun Yat-sen

To unite a country divided by warlordism, Sun resolved to march from his southern Guangdong stronghold north to the capital of Beijing. In a tragic twist of fate, however, Sun would not live to see his nation-building dreams come true. He died of cancer in 1925, leaving his life's work incomplete. Yet a momentous legacy lives on: Nationalists in Taiwan remember him as a founding father; Communists consider him a forerunner of the revolution against imperialism. To this day, Sun Yat-sen is one of the few political figures to represent the common ground on both sides of the Taiwan Strait.

Let's Get Ready to RUMBLE!

It was to be a David-versus-Goliath battle, as historian Laszlo Montgomery called it in his *China History Podcast*. In the spirit of Laszlo's colorful assertion, we now go live, ringside, for the announcement of the Fight of the Century:

> In the white corner...standing five feet, seven inches (169 cm) and fighting for the Chinese Nationalists, born in Zhejiang to a family of merchants, former commandant of the Whampoa Military Academy, fresh off his major victory over the warlords in the Northern Expedition, and the new President of the Republic, the Generalissimo, Chiang Kai-shek!

And in the red corner...standing five feet, eight inches (172 cm) and fighting for the Chinese Communists, born in Hunan to a family of farmers, known as a teacher, a poet, and a prolific labor organizer, previously a Nationalist Party Member, now Commander-in-Chief of the Red Army, Mao Zedong!

Mao Zedong (毛泽东, *Máo Zédōng*, 1893–1976) was the underdog by a long shot. Outgunned and undermanned, the Red Army relied on confiscation and redistribution of wealthy landowner assets, Robin Hood-style, to fund itself. Meanwhile, Chiang Kai-shek (蒋介石, *Jiǎng Jièshí*, 1887–1975) was well-funded and well-supplied, stepping into Sun Yat-sen's power vacuum with a massive army. The Generalissimo even had an air force, plus strategic guidance from German military advisors. His stated aim was to finish off the "communist bandits," then take on the much stronger Japanese army encroaching on northeast China, a fearsome battle he hoped to delay. A staunch Confucian who militarized Chinese society, Chiang distrusted foreign ideas like communism so much that he was willing to decimate great swaths of population to rid China of such influences. He once quipped, "The Japanese are a disease of the skin; the Communists are a disease of the heart."

In 1927, Chiang joined forces with Shanghai crime kingpin "Big Ears" Du Yuesheng and his Green Gang to eliminate thousands of Communist workers in the brutal Shanghai Massacre. During the next twelve months, over 300,000 people died across China in anti-Communist campaigns, at Chiang's command. Chiang spent eight more years trying to eradicate the Communists, his forces at times outnumbering the enemy by ten-to-one or even twenty-to-one.

All the while, Mao's message of hope was starting to resonate with the masses. Mao was a historian. He'd seen too many injustices over the course of history and in his own time, and he saw communism as a way out. His vision for China offered an escape from crushing taxation and the downward economic spiral enforced by the landed gentry and their exploitive militias, if only the Reds could survive the Nationalist onslaught.

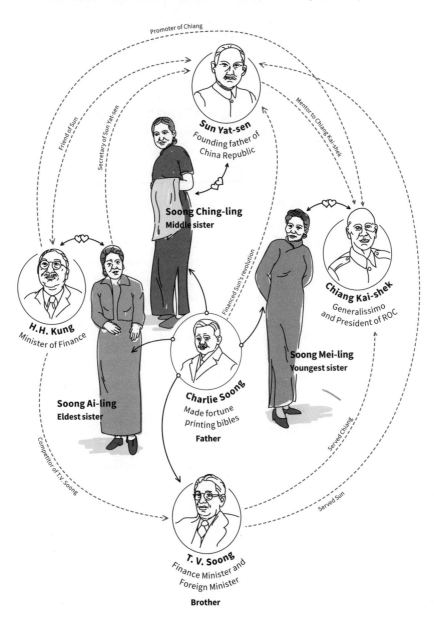

In his fifth and final campaign in 1934, Chiang mobilized a million-soldier army to encircle and lay siege to the Red Army in Jiangxi Province. Mao and the central Red Army escaped to trudge an astonishing 7,500 miles (12,070 kilometers), over twice the width of the North American continent, twisting northwest through rugged terrain to Yan'an. What started as a mass retreat was transformed into a victory of the spirit. It was a major badge of honor for the few who evaded capture or starvation. The year-long trek went down in history as "The Long March." Mao biographer Edgar Snow, in his classic *Red Star Over China*, was less coy, calling it "the biggest armed propaganda tour in history." It was along this journey that Mao Zedong—surrounded by an aura of invincibility, having never been wounded—ascended to a position of leadership. Chiang placed a quarter-of-a-million silver-dollar bounty on his head.

After the Long March, Snow spent time with the Red Army in Yan'an and observed the pervasive optimism of the unpaid rank-and-file soldiers, many still in their teens. The soldiers slept in caves or on open ground, sang songs and put on plays, and overflowed with a deep abiding belief they were building something much bigger than any of them. Snow reflected: "One felt that whatever there was extraordinary in this man grew out of the uncanny degree to which he synthesized and expressed the urgent demands of millions of Chinese, and especially the peasantry."

The Sino-Japanese War...Take Two

China's War of Resistance against Japan (1931–1945) intensified when Chiang decided to fight the Japanese instead of the Communists. This monumental decision came after he was kidnapped and held hostage in Xi'an, forced to reconsider a Nationalist/Communist united front, and concluded Stalin and the Soviets would likely support him.

The Marco Polo Bridge outside Beijing was the flash point. Japan's headstrong generals acted without government consent to take Beijing and Tianjin, with boasts of swallowing the whole of China in just three months. In Shanghai, Chiang engaged the Japanese in the largest land battle since the First World War, which fully awakened the fighting spirit of the Chinese nation. After many casualties on both sides, and wave after wave of Japanese reinforcements over three months, the Nationalists were forced to retreat. First Shanghai fell, then the capital of Nanjing. Over six weeks in late 1937, Japanese soldiers looted the capital and slaughtered its people in what has become known as the "Rape of Nanjing."

Two years later Germany invaded Poland to spark the conflict in Europe. Jewish refugees streamed into Shanghai and packed the Hongkou ghetto. In the wake of their retreat to the inland stronghold of Chongqing, a desperate Chiang ordered troops to burst dams and destroy infrastructure to frustrate Japan's plans for a quick victory. Japanese generals resorted to indiscriminant civilian bombing and the use of chemical and biological weapons, invoking horrors on the Chinese population. But Chiang held tight and drew on limited American military and financial aid. U.S. Army General "Vinegar Joe" Stillwell hated Chiang, whom he called "Peanut," but praised his troops: "The Chinese soldier best exemplifies the greatness of the Chinese people—their indomitable spirit, their uncomplaining loyalty, their honesty of purpose, their steadfast perseverance."

Soong Mei-ling, Chiang's elegant and eloquent wife, a "Fashion Icon" herself, took a leading role in Nationalist politics and became a popular overseas spokesperson who appeared three times on the cover of Time Magazine.

In 1945, the U.S. Air Force destroyed 68 Japanese cities, but there was still no capitulation. Only after atomic bombs were dropped on Hiroshima and Nagasaki did Emperor Hirohito broadcast his surrender speech. Oxford historian Rana Mitter reminds us that China, the "forgotten ally" of the Americans, British, French, and Russians, was first to fight in World War II, and with scant resources held down 600,000 Japanese troops. It was an important contribution to the overall Allied victory.

> *"We have always said that the violent militarism of Japan is our enemy, not the people of Japan. Although the armed forces of the enemy have been defeated and must be made to observe strictly all the terms of surrender, yet we should not for a moment think of revenge or heap abuses upon the innocent people of Japan."*
>
> — Chiang Kai-shek
> (victory speech in 1945)

Unfortunately, the victorious Chiang was unable to unite his country. Many of Chiang's local officials were still seen as corrupt thugs, or worse, former colluders with the Japanese. According to historian Jonathan Fenby, "Their claim to the mandate to rule was fatally undermined by their inability to offer a convincing new form of national government." When full civil war broke out in 1946, Mao's Red Army, which had suffered far fewer casualties in their guerrilla campaigns against the Japanese, drew upon a groundswell of public support to score a stunning victory over the Nationalists. Soldiers still loyal to Chiang retreated en masse with him to Taiwan, which prompted many in the West to ask, "Who lost China?" and set the stage for the complex ongoing relationship between the U.S. and Taiwan. Three decades later, in the 1970s, Chiang ceded power to his son, Chiang Chingkuo, who led the charge and oversaw Taiwan's boom to become one of Asia's "four little dragons."

THE FASHION ICONS

Sun Yat-sen's original suit made a lasting statement in China and beyond.

1910s Sun and his revolutionaries introduce their new style with the founding of the Republic.

1920s With Sun's death, followers attach more symbolic significance to the suit (see below).

1930–40s Mao, Chiang and Deng don the suit showing unity against the Japanese.

Intended to help them stand apart from the imperial Manchus, the suit combines German military and Japanese cadet uniform influences, along with Sun's own creative input.

Five front buttons = Five branches of government

Four pocket buttons = Four virtues for people to follow

Three cuff buttons = Three principles of nationalism, democracy, and people's welfare

Seamless back = Peaceful reunification

 Indigo blue Peasants and workers

 Khaki green Army officers

 Grey barathea Party cadres

Serve the People

Mao Zedong stood on the platform in Tiananmen Square on October 1, 1949, cheered by a million-plus throng of supporters to declare the birth of the People's Republic of China. The Chairman and his inner circle—Liu Shaoqi, Peng Dehuai, Lin Biao, and Zhou Enlai—were finally free of imperial rule and foreign domination, ready to pursue their egalitarian dream in the Motherland. A majority of the CCP leaders, who had been educated overseas, wanted China to emulate the Soviet model. Mao, on the other hand, argued for more homegrown influences.

Before Mao could get started, his country was pulled into a war across the border. China helped the North Koreans battle the U.S.-backed South Koreans to a stalemate. And then, in 1953, Mao instituted his First Five-Year Plan. It initiated many positive changes: an industrial push to rebuild the nation; language reform and character simplification which reduced illiteracy from eighty percent to thirty percent, and statutes to eliminate prostitution and concubinage. He recognized women as critical to China's future success and declared, "women hold up half the sky." Thousands of Chinese scientists and intellectuals returned from overseas to play a role in China's renaissance.

> *"The socialist system will eventually*
> *replace the capitalist system;*
> *this is an objective law independent of man's will.*
> *However much the reactionaries try to hold back*
> *the wheel of history, sooner or later revolution*
> *will take place and eventually triumph."*
>
> — Mao Zedong

Mao's vision went far beyond simply realizing a Communist utopia in China; he saw himself as the torch-bearer of a socialist world revolution, the heir apparent to Joseph Stalin, who had blown it by supporting Chiang over him. Neither Stalin nor his successor, Nikita Khrushchev, gave Mao any face. What's more, Khrushchev lost his street cred in China by denouncing Stalin's brutal record. Mao saw the Russians as slacking on the revolution. The world lacked a leader who could do justice to Marxist-Leninst ideals. Mao believed he could fill that void.

Leap Before You Look

The Great Leap Forward (1958–1961) was a gambit to catapult an agrarian China into the industrial big leagues. The concept was simple: nationalize the country's assets, centralize all the planning, then shift the people's energy towards steel production. Ambitious slogans such as, "Surpass the U.K. and the U.S. in three years!" and, "If our one day equals their twenty years, our shared dream will appear!" fueled everyone with enthusiasm. Flush with confidence, everyone set out to make it happen.

As the Chairman toured the nation by train to survey the Great Leap's presumed successes, officials greeted him with overstated evidence of plentiful harvests and massive jumps in production. His dreams of national self-sufficiency appeared within reach.

Based on these false reports and many like it, citizens were told to remove their home kitchens, since communal centers could now feed them for the rest of their lives. The 1958 harvest was good, but with many able-bodied farmers busy producing steel, much of the grain rotted in the fields. China continued exporting grain to Russia, even during the disastrous bad weather years of 1959–1961. Pair that with inaccurately reported crop totals, *et voilà*, instant catastrophic famine with massive casualties.

Revolution Reprised

Several years of economic recovery put China on a stable trajectory, thanks to reformers Liu Shaoqi and Deng Xiaoping.

China exploded a bomb over the Gobi desert in 1964 and became the fifth member of the nuclear club. Enter the Great Proletarian Cultural Revolution (1966–1976).

It's no secret this was a time of extreme turbulence and remains a very sensitive topic. In the end, many people who lived through it longed to recoup these lost years of their lives. To others, this reprised revolution was when they felt most alive.

Socialism with Chinese Characteristics

Deng Xiaoping (邓小平, *Dèng Xiǎopíng,* 1904–1997) launched his Reform and Opening Campaign in 1978 to jumpstart the Chinese economy. He called a truce in the war on Chinese tradition, and put economic prosperity ahead of political reform. The challenges ahead included a particularly tall order: regaining the trust of the outcast scientists, economists, managers, and intellectuals discredited during the Cultural Revolution. Deng encouraged everyone to act on their own initiative, in a grand experiment referred to as "crossing the river by feeling for the stones." He neutralized his leftist opponents with the dictum, "We regard reform as revolution."

Deng unleashed China's coastal economy by carving out Special Economic Zones to pursue market-oriented policies and attract foreign expertise and capital. As China continued its policy of opening to the West, direct foreign investment increased to an average of $35 billion per year from 1992 to 1999. Deng then used China's foreign obligations to sell through his more controversial domestic reforms. Deng biographer and Harvard professor Ezra Vogel writes that Deng urged all his officials to be bolder and try harder, to experiment, to take risks, and to not be afraid of making mistakes. He acknowledged that people in Guangdong and Fujian might get rich first, but they would then help other areas get rich too. To find structural changes of this magnitude in China, you'd have to go back two thousand years to the prosperous Han Dynasty. Deng and his followers succeeded in lifting 650 million people out of poverty over three decades—that's over 80% of the total number of people worldwide estimated to have been lifted

VIRAL MARKETING: THE LITTLE RED BOOK AS A CASE STUDY

Quotations from Chairman Mao (毛主席语录, *Máo Zhǔxí Yǔlù*) started as an internal military handbook, then morphed into a blockbuster advice guide. Let's investigate how the "Mao brand" evolved from inception to its peak of popularity:

1931 / Brand Soft Launch
Mao Zedong proclaimed Chairman of the Council of People's Commissars of the Soviet Republic of China, and later, Chairman of the Politburo, Chairman of the Military Commission, Chairman of the Communist Party, and so on.

1934 / Brand Enhancement
Mao consolidated power and built key alliances in the crucible of the Long March. Subsequent victories over the Japanese and the Nationalists added to his aura of invincibility, as a soldier immune to injury.

1949 / Brand Launch
Chairman Mao takes center stage at Tian'anmen Square on October 1, 1949 to found the People's Republic of China. Over 300,000 people gather, hoping to catch of a glimpse of him.

1964 / Product Test Marketing
The People's Liberation Army internally circulates *200 Quotations From Chairman Mao*. With Mao in semi-retirement and his comrades running the show, this publication refreshes his most memorable sayings within the hearts and minds of the PLA.

1966 / Product Wide Launch
The "Little Red Book" (LRB) with 427 quotations is published with the goal of reaching 99% of the population. On October 1, 1966, 1.5 million people (up 5x from 1949) gather in Tian'anmen, almost everyone holding the LRB.

1967 / Product Cult Status
Mao mania explodes during the Cultural Revolution. With over 700 million copies in print, the LRB helps people to tell friends from enemies. Even brides-to-be quote Mao before saying "I do."

1976 / Brand Legend Phase
At the time of Mao's death, the LRB was published in over 50 languages. Total copies in print copies later exceed 5 billion, drawing comparisons with the number of printed Bibles.

1979 / Product "Classic" Category Shift
As Deng Xiaoping's reforms gain momentum, the Party stops distribution, noting that the LRB had "mistakenly torn Mao's thoughts into misleading fragments." Almost overnight the title disappears from bookstores and reappears in antique shops.

out of poverty over that time period. Deng passed away before he could witness China's 2001 landmark entry into the World Trade Organization and the modern nation's debut at the 2008 Beijing Olympics. Centuries from now, experts will point to this time as one of the most incredible transformations in Chinese history.

"Modernization is at the core of all major tasks because it is the essential condition for solving both our domestic and external problems. Everything depends on our doing our work in our country well. The role we play in international affairs is determined by the extent of our economic growth."

— Deng Xiaoping

In 1990, China produced less than 3% of global manufacturing output; by 2015, it produced nearly 25%. Jonathan Fenby writes, "China's leaders still call themselves communists after a dazzling display of capitalism featuring private property, corporate shareholders and state-owned firm layoffs, resulting in an economy that has grown fourteen fold since reforms were launched in 1978."

TWELVE

Dragon in the Spotlight

Thanks for coming; we've got it from here

"China is as though ancient Rome was never dissolved and continued to the present day."

— Zhang Weiwei

"China is a big country, inhabited by many Chinese."

— Charles de Gaulle

Beyond the country's nearby Asian neighbors, with whom China shares many legacies and simmering disagreements, lie wastelands of hooligans with ample proboscis. This land is known as "the West." Endless numbers of their most curious do-gooders perpetually come to China with all the answers to her problems, both real and imagined. And while the Chinese welcome friendship and trade, showing great patience even with foreigners coming for the sole purpose of striking it rich, they're less patient with shoot-from-the-hip advice from outsiders when it comes to their own history and culture. After all, we're talking about the world's oldest living civilization.

> *"Patriots say Chinese love peace.*
> *But I don't understand,*
> *how can we have nonstop domestic*
> *wars while loving peace?*
> *Maybe this saying should be amended:*
> *Chinese want peace with foreigners."*
>
> — Lu Xun

This is not to eulogize China's past. It is rather to acknowledge that a modest understanding of China's intricate history enables us to avoid snap judgments and to perceive the unfolding events of the 21st century within the nation's broader historic context. How modern Chinese see themselves and their culture is profoundly shaped by the ideas and institutions created during their collective past.

Asia Society scholar Orville Schell observes, "To the great perplexity of many Chinese (especially officials), their country's extraordinary progress toward 'wealth and power' has not in itself managed to deliver the full degree of admiration that they once imagined these heroic accomplishments would automatically confer, and which they fiercely feel to be rightfully theirs." They performed an economic miracle, yet at times, confidence levels still lag their actual achievements. Schell continues, "Despite

China's enormous progress, a humiliation complex still remains, nationalism is still on the rise, and Chinese still so easily tend to feel victimized."

Chinese leadership has committed itself to regain this confidence and pride. "Habits of mind and of statecraft are as deeply ingrained in China as they are in the West, if not far more so, given the longevity of China's political culture," notes author Howard French. Beijing's push to establish its own set of institutions and initiatives, with itself as the central player, suggests a renewed cultural self-confidence and a fundamental belief that "as China gradually but inevitably becomes number one, other countries including the United States will slowly come to appreciate that resistance is pointless and will petition for admission into the Chinese court."

Unprecedented Prosperity, Unparalleled Challenges

China's return to its traditional Middle Kingdom role, with an end-of-century economic output of perhaps double or triple that of the U.S, is far from guaranteed. A recent Pew Research Center survey reveals the top concerns among China's own citizens: corruption, air and water pollution, widening inequality, crime, rising prices, food safety, and more. A daunting list indeed, though the majority of Chinese see these problems as improving over the next five years. What's more, over three-quarters believe their family is better off today than they were five years ago. And nearly all Chinese say their current standard of living is better than their parents' standard of living at the same age.

"China is standing before a critical crossroads, where reforms are as difficult as they are necessary. The more that progress is delayed, the harder it becomes."

— Zhou Qiren

Aye, there's the rub. In the past two centuries, the last thirty years has been the only extended period without war, famine or mass persecution, a period in which everyone's lives have been getting better and better. Expectations are now very high. And resistance to reform is intensifying, particularly among those who benefit most from the status quo.

China's leaders also face an aging crisis. Economists project the number of Chinese older than 65 will rise from roughly 100 million in 2005 to more than 329 million in 2050 — more than the populations of Germany, Japan, France, and Britain combined — making China one of the older societies in the world. China's Baby Boomer generation, the world's largest by number, has already started to retire. The younger generation of workers poised to take over is relatively small in number, a legacy of the nation's "One Child" policy from 1978 to 2015. This perfect storm of adverse demographics, plus skyrocketing retirement and health care costs, means the country may get old before it gets rich. If the current trends of reduced fertility and modest immigration continues, by the end of the 21st century, China's population will dip below one billion people (India will easily overtake them) for the first time since 1980. This reality has led some Chinese experts to conclude that the country's economic output may never reach its full potential. The economic chasm between the haves and have-nots may widen. History has shown us what happens when increasing numbers of a well-educated but disillusioned youth lose confidence in the future.

Socialist cadres banter about historian Alexis de Tocqueville's observation that a nation is not unstable when it's poor, but rather, when the government suddenly relaxes its pressure. This explains why the powers that be have doubled down on their communist origins while reconnecting with their traditional Chinese roots. Officials now quote Confucius, whose legacy Mao sought to eradicate, even as they celebrate the successes of the socialist market economy. China's reputation as a land of contradictions has never been more apparent.

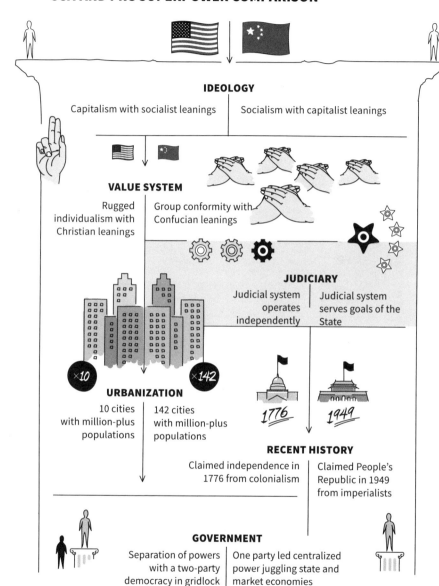

MATERIALISM

Widespread desire to get rich quick | Widespread desire to get rich even quicker

NARRATIVE

Patriotism wielded as a unifying force, i.e. Support Our Troops | National pride wielded as a unifying force, i.e. the China Dream

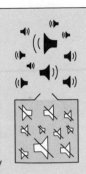

PUBLIC VOICE

Freedom of speech often used insensitively | Censored media with plenty of sensitivities

PERSONAL WEALTH

Widening gap between haves and have-nots | Widening gap between haves and have-nots

GREATEST FEAR

Democracy struggles, government turns authoritarian. | Authoritarianism struggles, society faces challenges.

GREATEST HOPE

Its best days are still to come | Its best days are still to come

People view them as total opposites, yet there is much in common.

Real Problems, Real Solutions

The dreams of most Chinese young men are modest: clean air, safe food, a decent job and an apartment of their own so they can attract a bride and get married. China already has the largest installed base of renewable energy (solar, wind, hydro) on the planet and is, ahem, waiting for more nations to show a similar level of commitment. Some enterprising Chinese who relocate to the West do so with a degree of hesitation, unwilling to declare their move as permanent.

> *"There is no such thing as what every Chinese thinks."*
>
> — Jeffrey Wasserstrom

Naysayers question how the enterprising spirit of the Chinese people can ever be liberated with a workforce educated for passivity and compliance. The answer: it's already happening. Those focused on the struggles of the debt-laden, state-owned enterprises miss the story of an exploding private sector that functions as a hyper-competitive breeding ground of fearless experimentation. In 2016, China became the first country to secure more than a million patent applications in a single year, which the World Intellectual Property Organization said reflected extraordinary levels of innovation. Management consultant Edward Tse, in his book *China's Disruptors*, employs the term "triple-jumping" in reference to entrepreneurs who leap competency gaps to create entirely new business ecosystems, as demonstrated by Pony Ma of Tencent and Ren Zhengfei of Huawei. On the whole, the Chinese people possess an uncanny ability to absorb change, accept the way things are, and get on with life. And, as author Peter Hessler notes, they don't try to make the world try to be like them.

> "If you don't give up,
> you still have a chance.
> Giving up is the greatest failure."
>
> — Jack Ma

The overseas Chinese diaspora of 46 million people also plays an important role, many with more than a passing interest in their culture and the ultimate fate of their ancestral home. From both within and without, the Chinese are solving their own problems, not waiting for anyone's help. A Chinese aphorism reminds us, those who say something cannot be done should not interrupt those doing it.

Our Interdependent Future

In his book *Clash of Civilizations*, Samuel P. Huntington argues that our inability to overcome cultural differences will increasingly lead to destabilization, and that an international order based on civilizations is the best safeguard against war. If we accept the spirit of Huntington's thesis, then we must ask ourselves: How can we create a common purpose among peoples from vastly different cultures?

There is reason for optimism: Research on the younger generation in China and the United States reveals that, rather than mirroring the generally negative views of the older generation, the youth of both nations hold quite favorable views of each other's countries and people. Born into prosperity, globally minded, and anticipating the future, perhaps their relative detachment from the tragedies of our 20th century will allow them to guide us forward towards cooperation in our 21st. As Einstein once said, the thinking that got us here isn't the thinking that can get us out.

Deng Xiaoping defined virtue as the courage to right past wrongs and embrace the ever-changing world. As human beings on this tiny planet in a vast cosmos, we are alive but for an instant.

In the words of the spiritual teacher, Ram Dass: "We are all just walking each other home."

> *"Our true nationality is mankind."*
>
> — H.G. Wells

Resources

Aisin-Gioro Puyi 爱新觉罗·溥仪. (2007). 我的前半生. 群众出版社.
Armstrong, Karen. (2006). *The Great Transformation: The World in the Time of Buddha, Socrates, Confucius and Jeremiah.* New York: Knopf Doubleday Publishing Group.
Ash, Alec. (2017). Wish Lanterns: *Young Lives in New China.* New York: Arcade Publishing.
Barrett, Timothy Hugh. (2012). *Taoism Under The Tang: Religion and Empire During a Golden Age of Chinese History* 唐代道教：中国历史上黄金时期的宗教与帝国. 齐鲁书社.
Bell, Daniel. (2008). *China's New Confucianism: Politics and Everyday Life in a Changing Society.* Princeton: Princeton University Press.
Bishop, Bill. (2015–2017). *Sinocism China Newsletter.*
Bouvet, Joachim 白晋(法). (2013). 康熙大帝. 黄慧婷译, 东方出版社.
Campbell, Joseph. (1988). *The Power of Myth.* New York: Doubleday.
Chang Kwang-chih 张光直. (2013). 中国青铜时代. 生活·读书·新知三联书店.
Chen Cunren 陈存仁. (2008). 被误读的远行. 广西师范大学出版社.
Chen Guying 陈鼓应. (1984). 老子注释及评介. 中华书局.
Chen Guying 陈鼓应. (1983). 庄子今注今译. 中华书局.
Chen Zhongtao 陈忠涛, Li Yanxiang 李彦祥. (2014). 难得有心郎：鱼玄机的诗与情. 中国言实出版社.
Coutinho, Steve. (2014). *An Introduction to Daoist Philosophies.* New York: Columbia University Press.
Du Yaxiong 杜亚雄. (2015). 中国民族器乐概论 (修订版). 上海音乐学院出版社.
Duanmu Cixiang 端木赐香. (2013). 1840：大国之殇. 当代中国出版社.
Durant, Will and Ariel. (2012). *The Lessons of History.* New York: Simon & Schuster.
Durant, Will. (1961). *The Story of Philosophy: The Lives and Opinions of the Greater Philosophers.* New York: Simon & Schuster.
Ebrey, Patricia Buckley. (2010). *The Cambridge Illustrated History of China, second edition.* New York: Cambridge University Press.
Fairbank, John King and Goldman, Merle. (2006). *China: A New History.* Cambridge, MA: The Belknamp Press of Harvard University Press.
Fallows, James. (2009). *Postcards From Tomorrow Square.* New York: Vintage Books.
Fenby, Jonathan. (2009). *The Penguin History of Modern China.* London: Penguin Books.
Fenby, Jonathan. (2014). *Will China Dominate the 21st Century?* Cambridge: Polity.
Feng Youlan 冯友兰. (2010). 中国哲学简史. 北京大学出版社.
Fish, Eric. (2016). *China's Millennials: The Want Generation.* New York: Rowman & Littlefield.
French, Howard. (2017). *Everything Under the Heavens: How the Past Helps Shape China's Push for Global Power.* New York: Knopf.

Fung Yu-lan. (1976). *A Short History of Chinese Philosophy.* New York: The Free Press.
Ge Jianxiong 葛剑雄. (2015). 葛剑雄写史：中国历史的十九个片断. 上海人民出版社.
Ge Jianxiong 葛剑雄. (2013). 统一与分裂——中国历史的启示. 商务印书馆.
Gescher, Jeanne-Marie. (2015). *All Under Heaven: China's Dreams of Order.* Kaduba House.
Giles, Herbert Allen. (2015). *China and the Chinese.* Hong Kong: Earnshaw Books.
Giles, Lionel. (2008). *The Art of War by Sun Tzu.* London: Masc. Hill.
Gu Hongming. (2013). *The Spirit of the Chinese People.* New York: CN Times Books.
Guo Jingyun 郭静云. (2013). 夏商周：从神话到史实. 上海古籍出版社.
Guo Moruo 郭沫若. (2010). 李白与杜甫. 中国长安出版社.
Hessler, Peter. (2009). *Oracle Bones: A Journey Through Time in China.* New York: Harper Collins.
Hinsch, Bret. (1990). *Passions of the Cut Sleeve: The Male Homosexual Tradition in China.* Berkeley, CA: University of California Press.
Hsu, C.Y. 徐中约. (2001). 中国近代史. Vol. 1, 香港中文大学出版社.
Huang Baosheng (2015). 黄宝生. 巴汉对勘<法句经>. 中西书局.
Huang, Ray. (1981). *1587 A Year of No Significance: The Ming Dynasty in Decline.* New Haven: Yale University Press.
Huang Renyu 黄仁宇. (2014). 万历十五年. 中华书局.
Huntington, Samuel P. (2007). *The Clash of Civilizations and the Remaking of World Order.* New York: Simon & Schuster.
Ivanhoe, Philip J. and Van Norden, Brian W. (2011). *Readings in Classical Chinese Philosophy, second edition.* Indianapolis: Hackett Publishing Company Inc.
Ivanhoe, Philip J. (2003). *The Daodejing of Laozi.* Translated by Ivanhoe P. J. Indianapolis, IN: Hackett Publishing Company Inc. and City University of Hong Kong.
Jenne, Jeremiah and Palmer, James. *Barbarians at the Gate* podcast. (2016–2017).
Jung Chang. *Empress Dowager Cixi.* New York: Knopf.
Keightley, David N. and Rosemont, Henry. (2014). *These Bones Shall Rise Again: Selected Writings on Early China.* Albany: SUNY Press.
Kissenger, Henry. (2011). *On China.* London: Penguin.
Koh Bee Yen. (2012). *Chinese Eminent People.* Singapore: Asiapac Books.
Kuo, Kaiser and Goldkorn, Jeremy. *The Sinica Podcast.* (2013–2017).
Lee, Ann. (2012). *What the U.S. Can Learn from China: An Open-Minded Guide to Treating Our Greatest Competitor as Our Greatest Teacher.* San Francisco: Berrett-Koehler Publishers.
Li Mengming 李孟明. (2014). 脸谱审美. 天津教育出版社.
Liang Congjie. (1996). *The Great Thoughts of China.* New York: John Wiley & Sons.
Lin Yanjiao 林言椒, 何承伟主编. (2009). 中外文明同时空：春秋战国vs希腊. 上海锦绣文章出版社.

Liu Yang. (2015). *East Meets West*. Mainz: Taschen.
Liu Yaru 刘雅茹. (2014). 竹林七贤. 文化艺术出版社.
Liu Yiqing 刘义庆. (2015).（南朝，宋）世说新语. 北京联合出版公司.
Lü Simian 吕思勉. (2014). 先秦史. 江苏人民出版社.
Ma, Damien and Adams, William. (2013). *In Line Behind a Billion People: How Scarcity Will Define China's Ascent in the Next Decade*. Upper Saddle River: Pearson FT Press.
Mair, Victor H. (2008). *The Art of War*. New York: Columbia University Press.
McGregor, James. (2012). *No Ancient Wisdom, No Followers: The Challenges of Chinese Authoritarian Capitalism*. Prospecta Press.
Menzies, Gavin. (2003). *1421: The Year China Discovered America*. New York: HarperCollins.
Meyer, Michael. (2010). *The Last Days of Old Beijing: Life in the Vanishing Backstreets of a City Transformed*. London: Walker Books.
Mitter, Rana. (2013). *Forgotten Ally: China's World War II, 1937–1945*. Boston: Mariner Books.
Montgomery, Laszlo. (2011–2017). *The Chinese History Podcast*.
Norell, Mark; Leidy, Denise Patry & The American Museum of Natural History with Ross, Laura. (2011). *Traveling the Silk Road*. New York: Sterling Signature.
Osnos, Evan. (2014). *Age of Ambition: Chasing Fortune, Truth, and Faith in the New China*. New York: Farrar, Straus and Giroux.
Pan, Lynn. (1984). *Old Shanghai: Gangsters in Paradise*. Singapore: Marshall Cavendish Editions.
Pan, Lynn. (1990). *Sons of the Yellow Emperor*. London: Mandarin Paperbacks.
Paulson, Henry M. (2015). *Dealing with China: An Insider Unmasks the New Economic Superpower*. New York: Twelve.
Peng Daya 彭大雅.（南宋）. 黑鞑事略. 维基文库.
Pillsbury, Michael. (2015). *The Hundred-Year Marathon: China's Secret Strategy to Replace America as the Global Superpower*. New York: Henry Holt & Company.
Plaks, Andrew. (1987). *Four Masterworks of the Ming Novel*. Princeton, NJ: Princeton University Press.
Pomfret, John. (2016). *The Beautiful Country and the Middle Kingdom: America and China, 1776 to the Present*. New York: Macmillan.
Polo, Marco. (2004). *Travels of Marco Polo., reissue edition*. New York: Signet.
Polo, Marco 冯承钧译. (2008). The Travels of Marco Polo. 江苏文艺出版社.
Roberts, J.M. and Westad, Odd Arne. (2004). *The Penguin History of the World, sixth edition*. London: Penguin Books.
Sagang, Secen. (2016). 萨冈彻辰（清）. 蒙古源流：蒙古族史籍. 道润梯步译校，中国国际广播出版社.
Schell, Orville and Delury, John. (2013). *Wealth and Power: China's Long March to the Twenty-first Century*. New York: Random House.
Seagrave, Sterling. (2010). *Lords of the Rim 2010: China's Renaissance*. Bowstring Books.
Shambaugh, David. (2013). *China Goes Global*. Oxford: Oxford University Press.
Shen Weibin 沈渭滨. (2007). 晚清女主：细说慈禧. 上海人民出版社.
Sima Guang 司马光（宋）. (2009). 资治通鉴. 中华书局有限公司.
Sima Qian 司马迁（汉）. (2006). 史记. 中华书局.

Snow, Edgar. (2007). *Red Star over China: The Classic Account of the Birth of Chinese Communism*. New York: Grove Press.
Song Yingxing 宋应星. (2008). 天工开物. 上海古籍出版社.
Spence, Jonathan. (2012). *The Search for Modern China*. New York: Norton.
Sui Lijuan 隋丽娟. (2007). 说慈禧. 中华书局.
Tan Shixiang 谭世骧. (1982). 中国历史地图集. 中国地图出版社.
The Chronicle of Chinese History. (2013). 中国历史年表. 中华书局.
Tian Hengyu. (2006). *Great Chinese Emperors*. Singapore: Asiapac Books.
Tse, Edward. (2015). *China's Disruptors: How Alibaba, Xiaomi, Tencent, and Other Companies are Changing the Rules of Business*. New York: Portfolio.
Vogel, Ezra. (2011). *Deng Xiaoping and the Transformation of China*. Cambridge: Harvard University Press.
Wang Enming 王恩铭. (2008). 美国反正统文化运动：嬉皮士文化研究. 北京大学出版社.
Wang Gungwu. (2014). *Another China Cycle: Committing to Reform*. Singapore: World Scientific Publishing.
Wasserstrom, Jeffrey. (2013). *China in the 21st Century: What Everyone Needs to Know*. Oxford: Oxford University Press.
Wasserstrom, Jeffrey. (2016). *Eight Juxtapositions: China Through Imperfect Analogies*. Penguin Specials.
Watson, Burton. (1993). Sima Qian's *Records of the Grand Historian: Han Dynasty*, revised edition. Translated by Watson, Burton. Hong Kong: The Chinese University of Hong Kong and Columbia University Press.
Weatherford, Jack. (2005). *Genghis Khan and the Making of the Modern World*. New York: Broadway Books.
Wells, H.G. (1961). *The Outline of History: The Whole Story of Man*. New York: Garden City Books.
Wen Yiduo 闻一多. (2009). 伏羲考. 上海古籍出版社.
Westad, Odd Arne. (2012). *Restless Empire: China and the World Since 1750*. New York: Basic Books.
Wilkinson, Endymion. (2015). *Chinese History: A New Manual*, Fourth Edition. Cambridge: Harvard University Asia Center.
Wu Gou 吴钩. (2015). 宋：现代的佛晓时辰. 广西师范大学出版社.
Wu Han 吴晗. (2013). 吴晗论明史. 武汉出版社.
Wu Han 吴晗. (2013). 朱元璋传. 湖南人民出版社.
Wu Renjing 吴仁敬. (2011). 中国陶瓷史. 团结出版社.
Xinran. (2008). *The Good Women of China: Hidden Voices*. New York: Anchor Books.
Xu Zhanquan 徐占权, Xu Jing 徐婧. (2001). 中国工农红军长征简史. 军事科学出版社.
Yang Jisheng. (2012). *Tombstone: The Great Chinese Famine, 1958–1962*. New York: Farrar, Straus and Giroux.
Yang Zengwen 杨曾文. (2014). 隋唐佛教史. 中国社会科学出版社.
Yu Hua. (2011). *China in Ten Words*. New York: Vintage.
Zhao Guangchao 赵广超. (2005). 大紫禁城, 王者的轴线. 三联书店（香港）有限公司.
Zheng Tianting 郑天挺. (2011). 清史探微. 北京大学出版社.
Zhu Naicheng 朱乃诚. (2009). 中华龙：起源和形成. 生活·读书·新知三联出版社.

References

All translations in this work are by the authors unless otherwise noted.

INTRODUCTION

"For Chinese people, history is our religion..." Zheng Wang. 16 June 2014. In China, 'History Is a Religion'. thediplomat.com/2014/06/in-china-history-is-a-religion/.

"The struggle of humanity against power..." BBC News. 10 Nov 2005. Ken Wiwa: 'Committed to remembering'. http://news.bbc.co.uk/2/hi/africa/4421188.stm.

"Those who question the present should investigate the past..." Liang Congjie. 1996. *The Great Thoughts of China*. New York: John Wiley & Sons. p. 97.

"So much of where we are..." Goodreads. (n.d.) William Langewiesche quotes. https://www.goodreads.com/quotes/60516-so-much-of-who-we-are-is-where-we-have.

CHAPTER ONE: DAWN OF THE MIDDLE KINGDOM

"If there are right men, then the government will prosper..." Liang Congjie. (1996). *The Great Thoughts of China*. New York: John Wiley & Sons. p. 86.

Yellow Emperor legends. Pan, Lynn. (1990). *Sons of the Yellow Emperor*. pp. 10–12. 袁珂 (2014). 山海经校注，北京联合出版社. Note: Sima Qian also opened his *Histories* with the story of the Yellow Emperor, and that's good enough for us.

Yu the Great legend. Ebrey, Patricia Buckley. (2010). *The Cambridge Illustrated History of China, second edition*. New York: Cambridge University Press. p. 10.

Oracle bone divination. Ebrey, Patricia Buckley. (2010). *The Cambridge Illustrated History of China, second edition*. New York: Cambridge University Press. pp. 21, 26.

Shang kings' rituals. Ebrey, Patricia Buckley. (2010). *The Cambridge Illustrated History of China, second edition*. New York: Cambridge University Press. p. 25. Note: The *shang* character in Shang Dynasty (Shāng Cháo, 商朝) is the same *shang* character used in business (shāngyè 商业).

Fuxi and Nuwa similar to Adam and Eve. 闻一多. (2009). 伏羲考，上海古籍出版社. Note: There are many legends about the mysterious origins of Fuxi and Nuwa, including this one which portrays them as brother and sister human progenitors.

China's bronze age started around 2000 BC. 郭静云. (2013). 夏商周：从神话到史实，上海古籍出版社.

The Mandate of Heaven. Fenby, Jonathan. (2009). *The Penguin History of Modern China*. London: Penguin Books. pp. 3–5.

Origin of the Middle Kingdom mindset. Ebrey, Patricia Buckley. (2010). *The Cambridge Illustrated History of China, second edition.* New York: Cambridge University Press. pp. 13, 31.

Greek *drakon* means "serpent." Ogden, Daniel. (2013). *Drakon: Dragon Myth and Serpent Cult in the Greek and Roman Worlds.* Oxford: Oxford University Press. p. 2.

Descendants of the Dragon. Hou Dejian. 侯德健 (1978年12月16日创作). 龙的传人，[新格唱片].

Forbidden City contains tens of thousands of dragons. 蒋蓝. (2012年第02期) "故宫瑞兽" 中国国家地理. www.dili360.com/ch/article/p5350c3da494ad92.htm

"Empty your mind. Be formless, shapeless, like water..." Absolute Motivation. (2014, August 24). The Wisdom – Bruce Lee. Youtube.com. www.youtube.com/watch?v=EPwQbQekk38. Note: Bruce Lee was born in the dragon year in the zodiac hour of the dragon and was nicknamed Little Dragon by his sister Agnes.

Dragon as a symbol of the Qing Dynasty. 朱乃诚. (2009). 中华龙：起源和形成，生活·读书·新知三联书店.

Chinese women gave birth to five percent more babies in 2012. BBC.com. (2012, January 23). Why China could see a dragon baby boom. www.bbc.com/news/av/world-asia-china-16675364/why-china-could-see-a-dragon-baby-boom

Singapore moms beat the average by ten percent. AFP News. (2012, January 22). *Singapore PM hopes for Year of the Dragon Baby Boom.* sg.news.yahoo.com/singapore-pm-hopes-dragon-baby-boom-063218694.html

CHAPTER TWO:
CHINA CATCHES THE SMART VIRUS

"How do I know that loving life is not a mistake?" Ivanhoe, Philip J. and Van Norden, Brian W. (2011). *Readings in Classical Chinese Philosophy, second edition.* Indianapolis: Hackett Publishing Company Inc. Kindle location 5008 of 8590 (chapter five, section two).

"Philosophy is the highest music." Durant, Will. (1961). *The Story of Philosophy: The Lives and Opinions of the Greater Philosophers.* New York: Simon & Schuster. Audiobook (introduction).

Confucius created a blueprint for restoring the golden age. Ivanhoe, Philip J. and Van Norden, Brian W., Kindle location 294 of 8590 (Introduction). Note: The name "Confucius" was a Jesuit creation in the 16th century.

"I am not someone who was born wise." Ebrey, Patricia Buckley. (2010). *The Cambridge Illustrated History of China, second edition.* New York: Cambridge University Press. p. 46.

"Generosity and kind words...are suitable everywhere." Kelly, John; Sawyer, Sue; and Yareham, Victoria. (2005). *Sigalovada Sutta: The Buddha's Advice to Sigalaka.* www.accesstoinsight.org/tipitaka/dn/dn.31.0.ksw0.html. Note: The exact birth dates for Buddha and Laozi are anyone's guess, e.g. Buddha may be (480–400BC) or (563–483BC).

"The business of a benevolent person..." Ivanhoe, Philip J. and Van Norden, Brian W. (2011). *Readings in Classical Chinese Philosophy, second edition.* Indianapolis: Hackett Publishing Company Inc. Kindle location 2341 of 8590 (chapter two, section 32).

"...the Way comprehends them as one." Ivanhoe, Philip J. and Van Norden, Brian W. (2011). *Readings in Classical Chinese Philosophy, second edition.* Indianapolis: Hackett Publishing Company Inc. Kindle location 4,934 of 8,590 (chapter five, section two).

"We survive in adversity..." "生于忧患,死于安乐..." 孟子. (2013). 孟子, 上海古籍出版社. Kindle location 3197 of 3921.

"Learning proceeds until death..." " 学至乎没而后止也..." 荀子. (2014). 荀子, 上海古籍出版社. Kindle location 143 of 8293.

Roger T. Ames on philosophers. Core Spirit. (n.d.) The Origins of Chinese Philosophical Thinking. www.corespirit.com/origins-chinese-philosophical-thinking.

"If you set an example by being correct..." Ivanhoe, Philip J. and Van Norden, Brian W. (2011). *Readings in Classical Chinese Philosophy, second edition.* Indianapolis: Hackett Publishing Company Inc. Kindle location 795 of 8590 (chapter one, book 12).

Confucius' four relationships. Wasserstrom, Jeffrey. (2013). *China in the 21st Century: What Everyone Needs to Know.* Oxford: Oxford University Press. pp. 2–3.

In Confucianism people are not equal. 秋风. (2014). 儒家式现代秩序, 广西师范大学出版社. Kindle location 1842 of 4040.

"Be all that you can be." Chambers, Mary Kate and Vergun, David. (2006, October 13). Army recruiting messages help keep Army rolling along. www.army.mil/article/322/army-recruiting-messages-help-keep-army-rolling-along/

"What you do not wish for yourself..." Note: interesting similarity between this quote and the Golden Rule articulated in the Bible in Matthew 7:12 and Luke 6:31. This "golden rule" concept can be found in nearly all belief systems.

"Do not be concerned that no one has heard of you..." Ivanhoe, Philip J. and Van Norden, Brian W. (2011). *Readings in Classical Chinese Philosophy, second edition.* Indianapolis: Hackett Publishing Company Inc. Kindle location 441 of 8590 (chapter one, book four). Note: The other Confucius quotes in this graphic also come from Ivanhoe and Van Norden.

Confucianism arose from certain economic conditions. Fung Yu-lan. (1976). *A Short History of Chinese Philosophy.* New York: The Free Press. pp. 21–22.

"When you observe goodness in others..." Ivanhoe, Philip J. and Van Norden, Brian W. (2011). *Readings in Classical Chinese Philosophy, second edition.* Indianapolis: Hackett Publishing Company Inc. Kindle location 5855 of 8590 (chapter six, section two).

The Five Punishments. Ivanhoe, Philip J. and Van Norden, Brian W. (2011). *Readings in Classical Chinese Philosophy, second edition.* Indianapolis: Hackett Publishing Company Inc. Kindle location 2518 of 8590 (chapter two, footnotes).

"Learning proceeds until death…" Ivanhoe, Philip J. and Van Norden, Brian W. (2011). *Readings in Classical Chinese Philosophy, second edition.* Indianapolis: Hackett Publishing Company Inc. Kindle location 5811 of 8590 (chapter six, section one).

Confucius' family tree in 83rd generation. China Economic Net. (2009, January 4). Confucius family tree revision ends with 2 mln descendants. http://en.ce.cn/National/culture/200901/04/t20090104_17866318.shtml

Confucius estimated number of descendants. Yan Liang (2008, February 16). Updated Confucius family tree has two million members. http://news.xinhuanet.com/english/2008-02/16/content_7616027.htm. Note: According to the Confucius Genealogy Compilation Committee, he has two million known and registered descendants, with an estimated three million in all.

Excessive desires are unnatural. Ivanhoe, Philip J. and Van Norden, Brian W. (2011). *Readings in Classical Chinese Philosophy, second edition.* Indianapolis: Hackett Publishing Company Inc. Kindle location 3720 of 8590 (chapter four, introduction).

The worst kind of virtue. Tierney, John. (2014, December 15). A Meditation on the Art of Not Trying. www.nytimes.com/2014/12/16/science/a-meditation-on-the-art-of-not-trying.html.

***Wuwei* as an antidote to paralysis by analysis.** Tierney, John. (2014, December 15). A Meditation on the Art of Not Trying. www.nytimes.com/2014/12/16/science/a-meditation-on-the-art-of-not-trying.html.

"One who believes everything in a book, would be better off without books." "尽信书不如无书." 孟子. (2013). 孟子，上海古籍出版社. Kindle location 3611 of 3921.

"A trap is for fish…" Ivanhoe, Philip J. and Van Norden, Brian W. (2011). *Readings in Classical Chinese Philosophy, second edition.* Indianapolis: Hackett Publishing Company Inc. Kindle location 5506 of 8590 (chapter five, section 26).

"Making a point to show that a point is not a point…" Ivanhoe, Philip J. and Van Norden, Brian W. (2011). *Readings in Classical Chinese Philosophy, second edition.* Indianapolis: Hackett Publishing Company Inc. Kindle location 5528 of 8590 (chapter five, section 2).

Krishnamurti's secret to life. Tolle, Eckhart. (2008). *The Journey into Yourself.* Eckhart Teachings, Inc. Audiobook.

Miles Davis philosophy of jazz. Moser, David. (n.d.) http://theanthill.org/jazz (inaccessible at time of publishing).

Sunzi as a legendary general. Note: There are many historians who consider Sunzi, like Laozi, to be a mythical figure whose writings were ascribed to him posthumously.

All warfare is based on deception. Giles, Lionel. (2008). *The Art of War by Sun Tzu*. London: Masc. Hill. Kindle location 92 of 757 (chapter one).

The large body of military lore attributed to "Master Sun." Mair, Victor H. (2008). *The Art of War*. New York: Columbia University Press. Kindle location 822 of 4340 (Introduction).

Warfare as analogous to persuasion. Combs, Steven C. (2000 August). "Sun-zi and the Art of War: The Rhetoric of Parsimony". *Quarterly Journal of Speech* Volume 86 Issue 3: pp. 276–294.

"All the sages preached a spirituality of empathy and compassion…" Armstrong, Karen. (2006). *The Great Transformation: The Beginning of Our Religious Traditions*. New York: Knopf Doubleday Publishing Group. Kindle location 127 of 9974 (Introduction).

"The inward life of man is exactly the same." Campbell, Joseph. (1988). *The Power of Myth*. New York: Doubleday. p. 170.

CHAPTER THREE:
YOU *CAN* TAKE IT WITH YOU

"The sage in governing the people…" Liang Congjie. (1996). *The Great Thoughts of China*. New York: John Wiley & Sons. p. 84.

"Give me a lever long enough…" Giga Quotes. (n.d.) Archimedes: Syracusan (Sicilian) geometrician. www.giga-usa.com/quotes/authors/archimedes_a001.htm

Seeing the Great Wall from the moon. López-Gil, Norberto. (2010, November 4). Is it Really Possible to See the Great Wall of China from Space with a Naked Eye? www.ncbi.nlm.nih.gov/pmc/articles/PMC3972694/

Battle of the Defense Systems. Pifer, Steven. (2015, March 30). The limits of U.S. missile defense. www.brookings.edu/opinions/the-limits-of-u-s-missile-defense.

Qin state considered most culturally backward. Ivanhoe, Philip J. and Van Norden, Brian W. (2011). *Readings in Classical Chinese Philosophy, second edition*. Indianapolis: Hackett Publishing Company Inc. Kindle location 2586 of 8590 (chapter two bibliography).

The Qin had long spears, layered armor and even crossbows. Montgomery, Laszlo. (2015, August 2). *China History Podcast*, episode 157.

The Qin intent to wipe out everyone who might later seek revenge. Montgomery, Laszlo. (2015, August 15). *China History Podcast*, episode 158.

Qin Shihuang built 4,250 miles of new roads. Montgomery, Laszlo. (2015, August 15). *China History Podcast*, episode 158.

"I am Emperor. My descendants will be numerous." Giga Quotes. (n.d.) The First Emperor of Qin. www.giga-usa.com/quotes/authors/qin_a001.htm.

Authorities prefer to wait to open Qin Shihuang's tomb. The Metropolitan Museum of New York. (2017, April 3). *Age of Empires: Chinese Art of the Qin and Han Dynasties*. Note: It's not about a fear of booby traps and rivers of poisonous mercury; experts are concerned about what might happen to the rare antiquities when exposed to air.

"**My father is your father, so go ahead…**" "吾翁即若翁…" 司马迁. (2006). 史记，中华书局. Kindle location 2239 of 21378.

The name of the Han ethnic group. Lü Simian 吕思勉. (2014). 先秦史，江苏人民出版社. Kindle location 404 of 8425.

CHAPTER FOUR: ANYONE HERE ORDER A CARAVAN OF SILK?

Chinese princess smuggles out silkworm eggs. 玄奘. (2008). 大唐西域记，陕西人民出版社，Kindle location 3891 of 3956.

Four Great Inventions altered the state of the world. Bacon, Francis. (2000). *The Instauratio Magna: Last Writings (The Oxford Francis Bacon)*. Gloucestershire: Clarendon Press. Note: Most Chinese scholars agree with Mr. Bacon.

Wudi liked to sneak out of the capital in disguise. 李彩煌. (2006). 秦汉三国皇帝传，百花洲文艺出版社. p. 134.

Sima Qian survived imprisonment to complete his *Shiji*. 司马迁. (2006). 史记，中华书局. Kindle location 21144 of 21379.

"I can imagine clothes made of silk…" Seneca the Elder. (1974). *Declamations, Volume I*. Cambridge, MA: Harvard University Press. p. 74.

Han Empire and Roman Empire comparison. 林言椒，何承伟主编. (2009). 中外文明同时空-秦汉vs罗马，上海锦绣文章出版社. pp. 58–59. Note: The West Han Empire near the end of Wudi's reign reached 6.2 million square kilometers. The Roman Empire didn't peak in size until Trajan's reign in 117–120 when it reached 5 million square kilometers. Some historians propose different measurements, but the general consensus is that the Han footprint was as big or bigger than the Roman footprint.

Cicero called Herodotus the "Father of History." Luce, T. James. (1997). *The Greek Historians*. New York: Routledge Publishing. p. 26.

Shiji was over half a million characters long. Knight, Sabina. (2013). *Chinese Literature: A Very Short Introduction*. Oxford: Oxford University Press. Audiobook.

Over 100,000 eunuchs in the Ming. Laven, Mary. (2013). *Mission to China: Matteo Ricci and the Jesuit Encounter with the East*. London: Faber & Faber. p. 116. Note: Some historians claim 70,000, some 100,000. Either way, it's an incredible number, with perhaps 10,000–15,000 of them working in the capital.

Eunuch Surgery, the gruesome truth. Jia Yinghua. (2008). *The Last Eunuch of China*. China Intercontinental Press.

Graham-Harrison, Emma. (2009, March 15) China's last eunuch spills sex, castration secrets. www.reuters.com/article/idINIndia-38511820090315.

"The long divided must unite…" 罗贯中. (2013). 三国演义，人民文学出版社. p. 1.

CHAPTER FIVE: NAKED IN THE WOODS

"If the Way is being realized in the world..." Ivanhoe, Philip J. and Van Norden, Brian W. (2011). *Readings in Classical Chinese Philosophy, second edition.* Indianapolis: Hackett Publishing Company Inc. Kindle location 612 of 8590 (chapter one, book eight).

"No one is free, even birds are chained to the sky." Goodreads. (n.d.) Bob Dylan quotes. www.goodreads.com/author/quotes/8898.Bob_Dylan

Shan Tao only wanting to be friends with Ji Kang and Ruan Ji. 刘义庆，南朝，宋. (2015). 世说新语，北京联合出版公司. Kindle location 3147 of 4184.

Lady Han observes Shan Tao and friends. Hinsch, Bret. (1990). *Passions of the Cut Sleeve: The Male Homosexual Tradition in China.* Berkeley, CA: University of California Press. p. 68. Note: According to Hinsch, the post-Han era is considered a high point in homosexual openness across all levels of society.

Liu Ling sings poetry and stumbles around naked. 刘雅茹. (2014). 竹林七贤，文化艺术出版社. p. 193.

"When I die, bury me with wine fermenting over my head." "死便埋我" 司马光. (2006). 资治通鉴，中华书局. Kindle location 19818 of 82297.

Ji Kang's letter to Shan Tao. 刘雅茹. (2014). 竹林七贤，文化艺术出版社. p. 256.

The Magic of Bamboo. Presentation Zen. (2010, July 23). Be like the bamboo: 7 lessons from the Japanese forest. www.presentationzen.com/presentationzen/2010/07/be-like-the-bamboo-trees-lessons-from-the-japanese-forest.html

Guinness World Records. (n.d.) First oil wells. www.guinnessworldrecords.com/world-records/first-oil-wells-.

Guinness World Records. (n.d.) Fastest growing plant. www.guinnessworldrecords.com/world-records/fastest-growing-plant.

Guinness World Records. (n.d.) Tallest bamboo. www.guinnessworldrecords.com/world-records/tallest-bamboo.

Newsweek. (2008, April 12). Stronger Than Steel. www.newsweek.com/stronger-steel-85533.

Smithsonian's National Zoo & Conservation Biology Institute. (2016, September 23). Giant Panda Update: A New Treat. nationalzoo.si.edu/animals/news/giant-panda-update-new-treat

MidAtlantic Bamboo. (n.d.) Bamboo is a grass. www.midatlanticbamboo.com/bamboo-tuf/tuf.htm

Ji Kang executed for perversion of public morals. Ebrey, Patricia Buckley. (2010). *The Cambridge Illustrated History of China, second edition.* New York: Cambridge University Press. p. 88.

Sui Dynasty endeavors to unify the country once again. Wang Gungwu. (2014). *Another China Cycle: Committing to Reform.* Singapore: World Scientific Publishing. p. 234.

CHAPTER SIX: POETS, PROPHETS AND PULCHRITUDE

Tang economy estimated at 60% of global GDP. Maddison, Angus. (2007). *Contours of the World Economy 1–2030 AD: Essays in Macro-Economic History.* Oxford: Oxford University Press.

Foreigners in the Tang legislative bureau. "近日中书尽是蕃人."孙光宪. (2013). 北梦琐言，浙江出版集团. Kindle location 422 of 1786. Note: Foreigners entering China during the Tang were mostly Persians, Arabs, Japanese, and Koreans.

An Arab earned the highest degree on the civil service exam. Baidu. (n.d.). "李彦升"baike.baidu.com/item/李彦升/4295129.

"The Way that can be expressed is not the everlasting Way…" Chen Guying 陈鼓应. (2003). 老子今注今译，商务印书馆. Kindle location 918 of 5429.

"The Way is beyond language…" Huang Baosheng 黄宝生. (2015). 巴汉对勘<法句经> 中西书局. p. 54.

Daoism and Buddhism received the most attention during the Tang. 杨曾文. (2014). 隋唐佛教史，中国社会科学出版社. Kindle location 3970 of 10498.

"How do you know it's not my fortune to meet the Son of Heaven?" Wikipedia. (n.d.) Wu Zetian. en.wikipedia.org/wiki/Wu_Zetian.

Wu Zetian accused Empress Wang of witchcraft. 司马光. (2016). 资治通鉴，中华书局. Kindle location 54469 of 82297.

Wu Zetian even strangled her own newborn daughter. 司马光. (2009). 资治通鉴，第2版. 中华书局有限公司. Kindle location 54,455 of 82,297.

"I need only three things to subdue a defiant horse…" 司马光. (2009). 资治通鉴，第2版. 中华书局有限公司. Kindle location 56,616 of 82,297.

Xuanzong kept tens of thousands of women. Wikipedia. (n.d.) Emperor Xuanzong of Tang. en.wikipedia.org/wiki/Emperor_Xuanzong_of_Tang. Note: "Yang Guifei" literally means "Consort Yang." Her birth name was Yang Yuhuan (杨玉环, Yáng Yùhuán). Yang became a consort after she returned from monastery and married Xuanzong.

Xuanzong and Yang Guifei one rocky separation after another. 司马光. (2006). 资治通鉴，中华书局. Kindle location 59494 of 82297.

Tang Dynasty census and An Lushan rebellion death toll. 司马光. (2009). 资治通鉴，卷二百二十三，唐纪三十九，第2版. 中华书局有限公司. Kindle location 61,676 of 82,297.

"I will not bow like a servant for five bushels of grain." 蔡日新. (2000). 陶渊明，知书房出版社. p. 53.

Du Fu and Li Bai poems. 雅瑟 (ed.). (2011). 唐诗宋词元曲大全，新世界出版社. Kindle locations 1806, 1243, 1379 of 8325.

Yu Xuanji poem. 陈文华、鱼玄机、李冶、薛涛. (2007). 梦为蝴蝶也寻花，上海古籍出版社，p. 92.

LinkedIn logo. LinkedIn. (n.d.) *"In"* symbol. www.linkedin.com.

CHAPTER SEVEN: WHY RULE WHEN YOU CAN BE AN ARTISTE?

"Whenever reading history..." Liang Congjie. 1996. *The Great Thoughts of China.* New York: John Wiley & Sons. p. 99.

Along the River has been called China's Mona Lisa. Bradsher, Keith. (2007, July 3). "China's Mona Lisa' Makes a Rare Appearance in Hong Kong." www.nytimes.com/2007/07/03/arts/design/03pain.html.

Along the River contained exactly 814 people. People's Daily Online. (2010, April 2). Qing Ming Shang He Tu (Along the River During the Qingming Festival/ Zhang Zeduan 12th century). http://english.peopledaily.com.cn/98669/99743/6939030.html. Note: "experts" have used other methods and reached the same count.

Pandas didn't appear in Chinese art until the 20th century. The Metropolitan Museum of New York. (2017, April 3). Age of Empires: Chinese Art of the Qin and Han Dynasties.

Printed money fueled transactions. Note: Cash was first introduced in China during the Tang, but mass printings in the Song caused a business upswing.

Song China's share of world population in 1100. Ebrey, Patricia Buckley. (2010). *The Cambridge Illustrated History of China, second edition.* New York: Cambridge University Press. p. 159.

China had little hope of regaining its dominance and swagger. Ebrey, Patricia Buckley. (2010). *The Cambridge Illustrated History of China, second edition.* New York: Cambridge University Press. p. 137.

Huizong's art collection comprised over 6,000 paintings. 孙汉慧. (2011). 宋徽宗赵佶的书画贡献, 吉林文史出版社. Kindle location 480 of 681.

Huizong produced over 15,000 paintings himself. 余辉. (2016). 宋徽宗花鸟画中的道教意识, www.sohu.com/a/78740531_424850.

"Peacocks move this way." 孙汉慧. (2011). 宋徽宗赵佶的书画贡献, 吉林文史出版社. Kindle location 561 of 681.

Huizong's foreign policy mistakes. Ebrey, Patricia Buckley. (2010). *The Cambridge Illustrated History of China, second edition.* New York: Cambridge University Press. p. 149.

Fundamentalism tends to thrive where people feel most threatened. Armstrong, Karen. (2007). *Islam: A Short History.* New York: Modern Library. Kindle location 2,412 of 3,232 (chapter five).

Neo-Confucian scholars influenced by Buddhist concepts. Wasserstrom, Jeffrey. (2013). *China in the 21st Century: What Everyone Needs to Know.* Oxford: Oxford University Press. p. 7.

Foot binding started in royal court. Fairbank, John King and Goldman, Merle. (2006). *China: A New History.* Cambridge, MA: The Belknamp Press of Harvard University Press. pp. 173–176.

The delicate Song female. Fairbank, John King and Goldman, Merle. (2006). *China: A New History.* Cambridge, MA: The Belknamp Press of Harvard University Press. p. 160.

Lines Written On A Summer's Day by Li Qingzhao. 周啸天. (1987). 唐绝句史, 重庆出版社. p. 369.

A prominent gynecologist called for removal of the clitoris. Wikipedia. (n.d.) Isaac Baker Brown. en.wikipedia.org/wiki/Isaac_Baker_Brown.

Precepts of Social Life. Fairbank, John King and Goldman, Merle. (2006). *China: A New History*. Cambridge, MA: The Belknamp Press of Harvard University Press. p. 107.

Yue Fei stories. All Empires History Forum. (2006, July 27). If not for General Yue Fei's Execution. www.allempires.com/forum/forum_posts.asp?TID=13620.

Genghis Khan's Y-chromosome. Callaway, Ewen. (2015, January 23). Genghis Khan's genetic legacy has competition. www.nature.com/news/genghis-khan-s-genetic-legacy-has-competition-1.16767.

Genghis Khan conquered more lands and peoples than the Romans. Weatherford, Jack. (2005). *Genghis Khan and the Making of the Modern World*. New York: Broadway Books. Audiobook.

The Mongol empire spanned the entirety of Asia. Norell, Mark; Leidy, Denise Patry; Ross Laura. (2011). *Traveling the Silk Road*. New York: Sterling Signature. p. 37.

An original Mongol population of fewer than 1.5 million people. Ebrey, Patricia Buckley. (2010). *The Cambridge Illustrated History of China, second edition*. New York: Cambridge University Press. p. 171.

Mongol women often ran the home affairs. Weatherford, Jack. (2005). *Genghis Khan and the Making of the Modern World*. New York: Broadway Books. Audiobook.

Voltaire called him the "king of kings." Weatherford, Jack. (2005). *Genghis Khan and the Making of the Modern World*. New York: Broadway Books. Audiobook.

Genghis Khan's secret grave. Steeds, Oliver. (2012, December 10). "The Hidden Grave of History's Greatest Warrior." Newsweek. pp. 20–28.

CHAPTER EIGHT: WHAT DOESN'T KILL YOU MAKES YOU STRONGER

"The weak fear the strong…" Yu, Hua. (2011). *China in Ten Words*. New York: Anchor Books. p. 143.

"Prosperity is not without many fears and distastes…" Brainy Quote. (n.d.) Francis Bacon Quotes. www.brainyquote.com/quotes/quotes/f/francisbac149819.html.

Kublai Khan's mother was a Nestorian and his favorite wife was a Buddhist. Weatherford, Jack. (2005). *Genghis Khan and the Making of the Modern World*. New York: Broadway Books. Audiobook.

Yuan Dynasty government was modeled on Chinese civil society. Tian Hengyu. (2006). *Great Chinese Emperors*. Singapore: Asiapac Books. p. 136.

Mongols great at war, bad at peace. Fairbank, John King and Goldman, Merle. (2006). *China: A New History*. Cambridge, MA: The Belknamp Press of Harvard University Press. p. 122.

Chinese citizens resented the Mongol presence. Fairbank, John King and Goldman, Merle. (2006). *China: A New History*. Cambridge, MA: The Belknamp Press of Harvard University Press. p. 118.

China flourished under Kublai's rule. Ebrey, Patricia Buckley. (2010). *The Cambridge Illustrated History of China, second edition*. New York: Cambridge University Press. p. 161.

Marco Polo visits China. Norell, Mark; Leidy, Denise Patry; Ross Laura. (2011). *Traveling the Silk Road.* New York: Sterling Signature. p. 39.
Ebrey, Patricia Buckley. (2010). *The Cambridge Illustrated History of China, second edition.* New York: Cambridge University Press. pp. 144, 161.

Zhu Yuanzhang, an overachieving peasant. 吴晗. (2013). 朱元璋传, 湖南人民出版社. Kindle location 2115 of 4115.

Protecting what was distinctly Chinese became a higher priority. Ebrey, Patricia Buckley. (2010). *The Cambridge Illustrated History of China, second edition.* New York: Cambridge University Press. p. 183.

CHAPTER NINE: THIS CHAPTER FOR MATURE AUDIENCES ONLY

"We shall not cease from exploration…" Goodreads. (n.d.) T.S. Eliot quotes. www.goodreads.com/quotes/9840.

"One cannot befriend a man who has no obsessions…" Ebrey, Patricia Buckley. (2010). *The Cambridge Illustrated History of China, second edition.* New York: Cambridge University Press. p. 203.

Ming exploration stopped. Fairbank, John King and Goldman, Merle. (2006). *China: A New History.* Cambridge, MA: The Belknamp Press of Harvard University Press. pp. 138–139.

Ming first dynasty to rule a united China from below the Yangzi River. Ebrey, Patricia Buckley. (2010). *The Cambridge Illustrated History of China, second edition.* New York: Cambridge University Press. p. 191.

Hongwu executed a total of 40,000 people. Fairbank, John King and Goldman, Merle. (2006). *China: A New History.* Cambridge, MA: The Belknamp Press of Harvard University Press. pp. 129–130.

Scholar arrives carrying his own coffin. Wikipedia. (n.d.) "钱唐" zh.wikipedia.org/wiki/钱唐.

The Four Great Novels. Plaks, Andrew. (1987). *Four Masterworks of the Ming Novel.* Princeton, NJ: Princeton University Press. pp. 497–498.

***Plum in the Golden Vase* as pornographic.** Li Wai-Yee. (2001). "Full-Length Vernacular Fiction," in Mair, Victor (ed.). *The Columbia History of Chinese Literature.* New York: Columbia University Press. pp. 640–642.

Forbidden City is among the world's most-visited tourist attractions. Travel + Leisure. (2014, November 10). The World's Most-visited Tourist Attractions. www.travelandleisure.com/slideshows/worlds-most-visited-tourist-attractions/17

Rocks sledded on ice to Beijing. Perkins, Sid. (2013, November 4). "Forbidden City Built from Stones Dragged on Ice." *Scientific American.* www.scientificamerican.com/article/forbidden-city-built-from-stone-on-ice/.

Ray Huang on highly stylized Ming society. Huang, Ray. (1981). *1587 A Year of No Significance: The Ming Dynasty in Decline.* New Haven: Yale University Press. p. 221.

CHAPTER TEN: MIND YOUR P'S AND QUEUES

"The wealthy vie with each other in splendor..." Fenby, Jonathan. (2009). *The Penguin History of Modern China*. London: Penguin Books. p. 681.

"Everything one does in life..." Brainy Quote. (n.d.) Jean Cocteau Quotes. www.brainyquote.com/quotes/quotes/j/jeancoctea141988.html.

Manchu society was based on hunting, fishing, and farming. Ebrey, Patricia Buckley. (2010). *The Cambridge Illustrated History of China, second edition*. New York: Cambridge University Press. p. 220.

First half of Qing was a high point of traditional Chinese civilization. Ebrey, Patricia Buckley. (2010). *The Cambridge Illustrated History of China, second edition*. New York: Cambridge University Press. p. 220.

"To keep your hair, you lose your head..." Zheng Tianting 郑天挺. (2011). 清史探微，第二版，北京大学出版社. Kindle location 852 of 6,798.

"Among those who realize the value of self-reflection..." 康熙. (2010). 庭训格言，中州古籍出版社. p. 23.

Kangxi pushed regents aside and took over at age 16. Koh Bee Yen. (2012). *Chinese Eminent People*. Singapore: Asiapac Books. p. 50.

Kangxi spent most of his spare time learning. Tian Hengyu. (2006). *Great Chinese Emperors*. Singapore: Asiapac Books. p. 163.

Kangxi avoided sensual overindulgence. Bouvet, Joachim 白晋 (法). (2013). 康熙大帝，东方出版社. Location 488 of 2,845. Note: Kangxi didn't exactly live a monastic life either. He kept more than 40 concubines in the palace, presumably to ensure he left a legacy for the empire.

Familiar pattern of Chinese history revisionism. Montgomery, Laszlo. (2015, August 2). *China History Podcast*, episode 157.

Barely 1% of Chinese could read or write. Jung Chang. (2013). *Empress Dowager Cixi*. New York: Knopf. p. 6.

"We possess all things..." Ebrey, Patricia Buckley. (2010). *The Cambridge Illustrated History of China, second edition*. New York: Cambridge University Press. p. 236.

China controlled one-third of the wealth in the 18th century. Osnos, Evan. (2014). *Age of Ambition: Chasing Fortune, Truth, and Faith in the New China*. New York: Farrar, Straus and Giroux. Kindle location 157.

Lords of the Rim. Seagrave, Sterling. (2010). *Lords of the Rim 2010: China's Renaissance*. Bowstring Books.

Manchus banned overseas migration. Pan, Lynn. (1990). *Sons of the Yellow Emperor*. London: Mandarin Paperbacks. p. 8.

Opium imports rose from 1,000 to 40,000 chests. Ebrey, Patricia Buckley. (2010). *The Cambridge Illustrated History of China, second edition*. New York: Cambridge University Press. p. 236.

Lin Zexu letter to Queen Victoria. Ebrey, Patricia Buckley. (2010). *The Cambridge Illustrated History of China, second edition*. New York: Cambridge University Press. p. 239.

The Great Divergence. Pomeranz, Kenneth. (2000). *The Great Divergence: China, Europe, and the Making of the Modern World Economy*. Princeton, NJ: Princeton University Press.

Hong Xiuquan son of God and younger brother of Jesus. Westad, Odd Arne. (2012). *Restless Empire: China and the World Since 1750*. New York: Basic Books. p. 47.

The Taiping took the lives of over 50 million people. 葛剑雄. (2010). 我们的国家：疆域与人口，复旦大学出版社. Kindle location 1490 of 1913. Note: Some scholars speculate China's population decline during the Taiping Uprising may have exceeded 100 million.

"This wonder has disappeared..." Jung Chang. (2013). *Empress Dowager Cixi*. New York: Knopf. p. 33.

Old Summer Palace eight times the size of Vatican City. Wikipedia. (n.d.) Old Summer Palace. en.wikipedia.org/wiki/Old_Summer_Palace.

Boxers United in Righteousness. Fairbank, John King and Goldman, Merle. (2006). *China: A New History*. Cambridge, MA: The Belknamp Press of Harvard University Press. pp. 230–231.

Westad, Odd Arne. (2012). *Restless Empire: China and the World Since 1750*. New York: Basic Books. p. 126.

"Oh, how magical it will be to have winter come every year." Goodreads. (n.d.) The Diary of Aisin-Gioro Puyi Quotes. www.goodreads.com/work/quotes/44501116-the-diary-of-aisin-gioro-puyi-the-last-emperor-of-china

CHAPTER ELEVEN: ENTER THE FASHION ICONS

"We must accept this modern civilization of the West..." Wang Gungwu. (2014). *Another China Cycle: Committing to Reform*. Singapore: World Scientific Publishing. p. 24.

"A handful of might is better than a bagful of right." Lubed Banana. (2013, July 6). The Fruit Chastity. http://lubedbanana.blogspot.com/2013/07/a-handful-of-might-is-better-than.html.

Many historians point to May 4 as the birth of modern China. Montgomery, Laszlo. (2011, June 15). *China History Podcast*, episode 046.

China sent 140,000 laborers to France to support the Allied war effort. Ebrey, Patricia Buckley. (2010). *The Cambridge Illustrated History of China, second edition*. New York: Cambridge University Press. p. 271.

Lu Xun's goal to bring out willpower in the Chinese people. Spence, Jonathan. (1982). *The Gate of Heavenly Peace: The Chinese and Their Revolution*. New York: Penguin Books p. 103.

Only 30 percent of China's troubles were caused by foreigners. Ebrey, Patricia Buckley. (2010). *The Cambridge Illustrated History of China, second edition*. New York: Cambridge University Press. p. 264.

Lu Xun quotes. Liang Congjie. (1996). *The Great Thoughts of China*. New York: John Wiley & Sons. Note: We considered the famous quote, "Chinese have never looked at foreigners as human beings. We either look up to them as gods or down on them as ghosts." However, we were unable to find the Chinese original to verify it came from Lu Xun.

Three Principles of the People. Montgomery, Laszlo. (2011, July 1). *China History Podcast*, episode 048. Note: Sun Zhongshan's birth name was Sun Wen. He picked up the name Sun Yat-sen at school in Hong Kong. The name Sun Zhongshan came later in Japan, as a derivation of his Japanese name.

"Comparing human and physical properties…" Liang Congjie. (1996). *The Great Thoughts of China*. New York: John Wiley & Sons. p. 185.

"Shanghai was where the modern world began…" Pan, Lynn. (2009). *Shanghai: A Century of Change in Photographs 1843–1949*. Hong Kong: Peace Book Co. Introduction.

"Japanese are a disease of the skin…" Montgomery, Laszlo. (2013, June 10). *China History Podcast*, episode 119.

Over 300,000 people died across China in anti-Communist campaigns. Wikipedia. (n.d.) Chiang Kai-shek. en.wikipedia.org/wiki/Chiang_Kai-shek.

Chiang's forces far outnumbered the Communists. Montgomery, Laszlo. (2013, June 10). *China History Podcast*, episode 119.

Mao and the central Red Army trudged 7,500 miles. 徐占权. (2005年第07期). "**长征到底有多长？**" *中国国家地理*. www.dili360.com/cng/article/p5350c3d82edf586.htm

The biggest armed propaganda tour in history. Snow, Edgar. (2007). *Red Star over China: The Classic Account of the Birth of Chinese Communism*. New York: Grove Press. Kindle location 3,212 of 10,563 (Part five, chapter four).

A quarter-of-a-million silver-dollar bounty on Mao's head. Snow, Edgar. (2007). *Red Star over China: The Classic Account of the Birth of Chinese Communism*. New York: Grove Press. Kindle location 491 of 10,563 (Part one, chapter one).

"One felt that whatever there was extraordinary in this man…" Snow, Edgar. (2007). *Red Star over China: The Classic Account of the Birth of Chinese Communism*. New York: Grove Press. Kindle location 1032 of 10,563 (part three, chapter one).

The U.S. Air Force destroyed 68 Japanese cities. Foreign Policy. (2013, May 30). *The Bomb Didn't Beat Japan…Stalin Did.* http://foreignpolicy.com/2013/05/30/the-bomb-didnt-beat-japan-stalin-did/.

"We have always said that the violent militarism of Japan is our enemy…" TV Tropes. (n.d.) Useful Notes / Chiang Kai-shek. http://tvtropes.org/pmwiki/pmwiki.php/UsefulNotes/ChiangKaiShek.

"Their claim to the mandate to rule was fatally undermined…" Fenby, Jonathan. (2009). *The Penguin History of Modern China*. London: Penguin Books. p. 674.

"The Chinese soldier best exemplifies the greatness of the Chinese people…" Perlez, Jane. (2016, February 23). China Maintains Respect, and a Museum, for a U.S. General. www.nytimes.com/2016/02/24/world/asia/chongqing-joseph-stilwell-museum.html.

Soong Mei-ling took a leading role in Nationalist politics. Karon, Tony. (2003, October 24). Madame Chiang Kai-shek, 1898–2003. http://content.time.com/time/world/article/0,8599,526008,00.html

Mao's language reforms reduced illiteracy. 苏培成. (2009年5月28日). 汉字进入了简化时代，光明日报.

The Fashion Icons' Sun Yat-sen suit influences. 陈蕴茜. (2007年9月). 南京大学学术月刊.

"The socialist system will eventually replace the capitalist system..." Liang Congjie. (1996). *The Great Thoughts of China.* New York: John Wiley & Sons. p. 100.

Khrushchev denounced Stalin's brutal record. MacFarquhar, Roderick. (2015, August 13). China: The Superpower of Mr. Xi. www.chinafile.com/library/nyrb-china-archive/china-superpower-mr-xi.

The Little Red Book. Mao Tsetung. (1972). *Quotations from Chairman Mao Tsetung.* Foreign Languages Press. Note: Those were turbulent times and many people suffered and died. Still, the Little Red Book provides an instructive example of viral marketing in the context of a mass movement.

Crossing the river by feeling for the stones. Osnos, Evan. (2014). *Age of Ambition: Chasing Fortune, Truth, and Faith in the New China.* New York: Farrar, Straus and Giroux. p. 14. Note: This expression originally came from Chen Yun.

"We regard reform as revolution." Wang Gungwu. (2014). *Another China Cycle: Committing to Reform.* Singapore: World Scientific Publishing. p. 212.

Direct foreign investment increased to $35 billion per year. Vogel, Ezra. (2011). *Deng Xiaoping and the Transformation of China.* Cambridge: Harvard University Press. Kindle location 14,001 of 22,539 (chapter 23).

China lifted 650 million people out of poverty. Li, Eric X. (2013, June). A tale of two political systems. www.ted.com/talks/eric_x_li_a_tale_of_two_political_systems.

"Modernization is the core of all major tasks..." Vogel, Ezra. (2011). *Deng Xiaoping and the Transformation of China.* Cambridge: Harvard University Press. Kindle location 7,406 of 22,539 (chapter 12).

China's global manufacturing output 1999–2015. The Economist. (2015, March 12). Made in China? www.economist.com/news/leaders/21646204-asias-dominance-manufacturing-will-endure-will-make-development-harder-others-made. p. 11.

"China's leaders still call themselves Communists..." Fenby, Jonathan. (2009). *The Penguin History of Modern China.* London: Penguin Books. p. 675.

CHAPTER TWELVE: DRAGON IN THE SPOTLIGHT

"China is as though ancient Rome was never dissolved..." Fallows, James. (2012). *China Airborne: The Test of China's Future.* New York: Vintage. p. 233.

"China is a big country…" O'Dwyer, Graham. (2017). *Charles de Gaulle, the International System, and the Existential Difference.* New York: Routledge. p. 130. Note: De Gaulle is often ridiculed for this remark, however, it was his attempt to talk directly to the Chinese individual, according to O'Dwyer: "To bring China back into the global community, to see past communism, and to see the ethno-symbolic essence of China."

"Patriots say Chinese love peace…" 鲁迅. (2013). 华盖集，译林出版社. Kindle location 730 of 1295.

"How modern Chinese see themselves…" Ebrey, Patricia Buckley. (2010). *The Cambridge Illustrated History of China, second edition.* New York: Cambridge University Press. p. 363. Note: Dr. Ebrey also wrote, "China is an extraordinarily complex society that has been in the making for several thousand years, and its present is not comprehensible without an understanding of its past."

"To the great perplexity of many Chinese…" Schell, Orville and Delury, John. (2013). *Wealth and Power: China's Long March to the Twenty-first Century.* New York: Random House. Kindle Location 6787 of 8633.

"Habits of mind and of statecraft are as deeply ingrained in China…" French, Howard. *Everything Under the Heavens: How the Past Helps Shape China's Push for Global Power.* Kindle location 4,493 of 5610.

"China is standing before a critical crossroads…" Fenby, Jonathan. (2014). *Will China Dominate the 21st Century?* New York: John Wiley & Sons. p. 124.

"There's no such thing as what every Chinese thinks." Wasserstrom, Jeffrey. (2012 September 21). On China's diversity. China Economic Review. www.chinaeconomicreview.com/china%E2%80%99s-diversity. Note: Professor Wasserstrom confirmed this anecdotal quote via email.

China first country to secure more than a million patent applications. *Financial Times.* (2016, November 24). China became the first country to secure more than a million patent applications. www.ft.com/content/4b6a9820-b210-11e6-a37c-f4a01f1b0fa1?mhq5j=e4.

Gratitude

We extend our heartfelt gratitude to the early reviewers who guided us and inspired us to persevere on our storytelling journey. Special thanks to Jesse Wu, Jonathan Seliger, Brantley Turner, George Bobyk, and Rudi Messner who commented on multiple versions and challenged us to refine our thinking. And much love to our heroic spouses, Kim and Shaoqing, who helped us keep the faith. Were it not for all this support, it's unlikely this book would be in your hands today.

Kudos to our talented project team: Yang Kanzhen for the book's beautiful illustrations, cover design, and logo; Alessandro Gottardo for his elegantly simple cover art; Chua Liwei for her research and content development; Yi Shun Lai for her adept editing; and Janine Milstrey for her sharp book layout. A special shout-out goes to Michael Colozzi, who dreamed up our "untangling the noodles" slogan. Thanks also to our friends at the China Institute and the Asia Society, including Tony Jackson who authored the foreword.

To our valued readers, we send our love and invite you to join us in the worldwide dialog towards cultural awareness and unity in diversity. Please take a moment to post a brief review of this book online, and share it with others. We look at, and learn from, every review.

About the Authors

Sun Zhumin 孙祝旻
is a passionate storyteller and translator in her native China. During the creation of this book, Zhumin had imaginary conversations with ancestors, received input from her two kids, and debated it with her history-buff husband.

Stewart Lee Beck 李渡
is a producer and author who's lived in China since 1992 and finds its people and culture endlessly fascinating. Stew refers to his Malaysian Chinese wife as "the crazy woman who keeps me sane."

Yang Kanzhen 杨侃真
is an elder twin and veteran graphic designer with a talent for simplifying the complicated and complicating the simple. Kanzhen illustrated this book and created the China Simplified noodle logo.

Interested in more from China Simplified?
Visit www.chinasimplified.com to get your copy of

China Simplified: Language Empowerment!

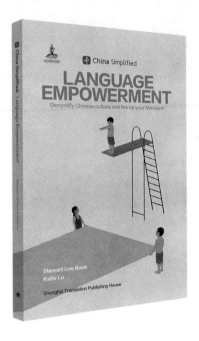

"I suddenly feel as if the scales have been lifted from my eyes. You truly demonstrate how understanding the language unveils so much about the culture."
— *Carol Potter, Executive Vice Chairman at Edelman*

"The authors are the grinning pilots who take you up in a plane for a good look at the lay of the land, and then ask you to jump!"
— *John Pasden, Founder and CEO, AllSet Learning*

"Reveals insights that many teachers and textbooks overlook. Recommended reading not only for language students, but also for anyone else who wants to understand how Chinese people think, act and talk."
— *Olle Linge, Mandarin Language Educator, Founder Hacking Chinese*

图书在版编目(CIP)数据

趣简中国史 = History Flashback: 英文 /（美）李渡（Stewart Lee Beck），孙祝旻著. —上海．上海译文出版社，2019. 10
（中国不简单）
ISBN 978 – 7 – 5327 – 8229 – 1

I. ① 趣… II. ① 李… ② 孙… III. ① 中华文化—介绍—英文
IV. ① K203

中国版本图书馆 CIP 数据核字（2019）第133455号

本书由国家出版基金资助出版

History Flashback
Authors: Stewart Lee Beck, Sun Zhumin
Illustrator: Yang Kanzhen
Editors: Rebecca Himpson, Yi Shun Lai
Executive Editor: Jin Yu
Cover Designers: Yang Kanzhen, Xu Xiaoying
Cover Art: Alessandro Gottardo
Typesetting: Red Cape Production

上海译文出版社有限公司出版、发行
网址：www.yiwen.com.cn
200001 上海福建中路193号
昆山市亭林印刷有限责任公司印刷

开本 889×1194 1/32 印张 7 插页 1 字数 279,000
2019年10月第1版 2019年10月第1次印刷
印数：0,001-5,000册

ISBN 978-7-5327-8229-1 / K·273
定价：55.00元

本书专有出版权归本社独家所有，非经本社同意不得连载、摘编或复制
如有质量问题，请与承印厂质量科联系，T: 0512-57751097